Avenues

Alfredo Schifini
Deborah J. Short
Josefina Villamil Tinajero

Erminda García
Eugene E. García
Else Hamayan
Lada Kratky

HAMPTON-BROWN

Grades 3–5 Curriculum Reviewers

Fran Alcántara
Bilingual Support Teacher
Cicero Public Schools District 99
Cicero, Illinois

Santina Y. Buffone, Ed.D.
Coordinator
Bilingual/Compensatory Education
Dearborn Public Schools
Dearborn, Michigan

Anastasia Colón
Bilingual Teacher
Buhrer Elementary
Cleveland Municipal School District
Cleveland, Ohio

Kelley E. Crockett
Team Leader, Language Center
Meadowbrook Elementar
Fort Worth Independent School
 District
Fort Worth, Texas

Marian Evans
Teacher
Ault Elementary
Cypress-Fairbanks Independent
 School District
Houston, Texas

David Garcia
Bilingual/ESL Teacher
Winston Elementary
Edgewood Independent School
 District
San Antonio, Texas

Sue Goldstein
*Bilingual Education Coordinator
 and Program Teacher*
Regional Multicultural Magnet School
New London, Connecticut

Sandra Guerra
Assistant Principal
Chapa Elementary
La Joya Independent School District
La Joya, Texas

Ruth Henrichs
ESL Teacher
Fleetwood Elementary
East Ramapo Central School District
Spring Valley, New York

Linda Hoste, M.Ed.
ESL Specialist
Birdville Independent School District
Fort Worth, Texas

Virginia Jama
ESL Coordinator, K–12
New York City Board of Education
Brooklyn, New York

Liliana Jaurrieta
Teacher
Lujan-Chavez Elementary
Socorro Independent School District
El Paso, Texas

Clara Levy
Teacher
Mesita Elementary
El Paso Independent School District
El Paso, Texas

Dr. Mark R. O'Shea
Professor of Education
Institute for Field-Based Teacher
 Education
California State University,
 Monterey Bay
Monterey, California

Lily Pham Dam
Former Administrator
Dallas Independent School District
Dallas, Texas

Raul Ramirez, Jr.
Bilingual/GT Teacher
Royalgate Elementary
South San Antonio
 Independent School District
San Antonio, Texas

Christa A. Wallis
*Elementary Program Specialist
 English Learners*
San Bernardino City Unified School
 District
San Bernardino, California

Acknowledgments

Every effort has been made to secure permission, but if any omissions have been made, please let us know. We gratefully acknowledge the following permissions:

Cover Design and Art Direction: Pronk&Associates.

Cover Illustration: Nadia Richie.

Charlesbridge Publishing, Inc.: "*The Ugly Vegetables*" by Grace Lin. Text copyright © 1999 by Grace Lin. All rights reserved. Used with permission by Charlesbridge Publishing, Inc.

Acknowledgments continue on page 499.

Hampton-Brown
P.O. Box 223220
Carmel, California 93922
800-333-3510
www.hampton-brown.com

Printed in the United States of America

ISBN 0-7362-1673-1

04 05 06 07 08 09 10 11 12   9 8 7 6 5 4 3 2

Avenues Go Everywhere

Unit 1

Community Counts

Social Studies
- Local Government
- Community Change

Unit 3

MOON LIGHT, MOON BRIGHT

Science
- The Moon
- The Solar System

CACTUS AND CANYONS

Social Studies
- Regions

Science
- Ecosystems

Nonfiction
Science Article

Fiction
Adventure Story

Eve Bunting's
WORLD OF STORIES

Social Studies
- Citizenship
- Immigration

Good for You!

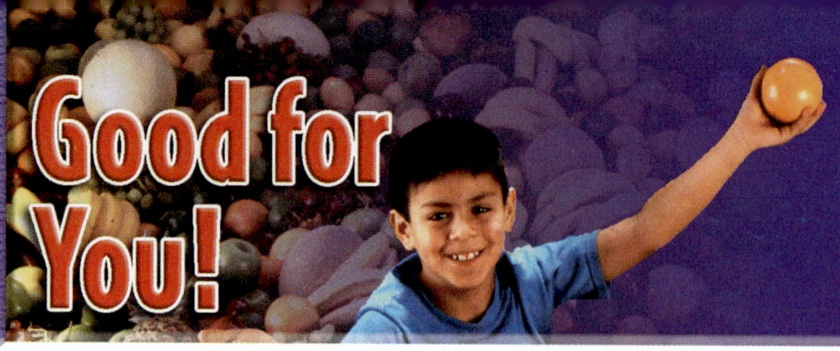

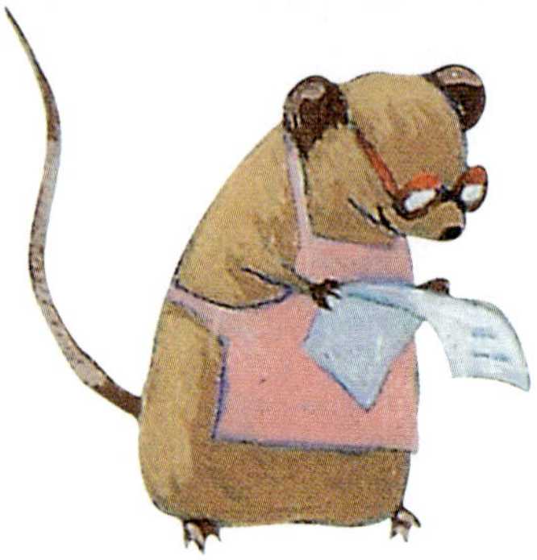

Science
- Nutrition
- Personal Health

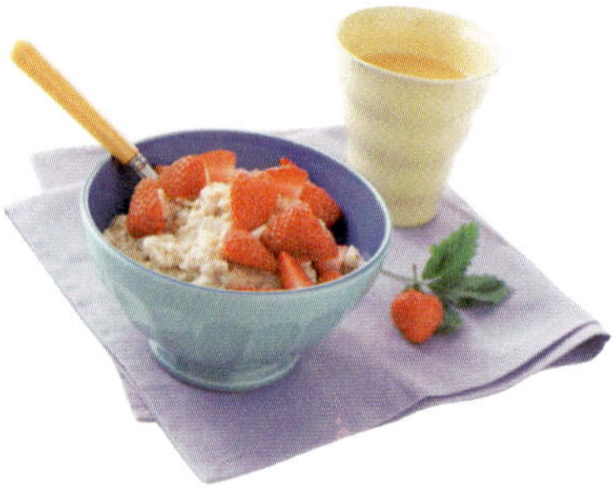

Community Counts

Map Your Community

1. Draw a place you like in your community.
2. Tell why you like it.
3. Work with your class. Put your drawings together to make a map of your community.

Royalgate Park/School

BathroomS

Royalgate Drive

Kinds of Communities

▲ An urban community is a city.

▲ A suburban community is outside a larger city or town.

▲ A rural area has few houses and a lot of land.

Community Government

mayor

▲ city council

BOSTON CITY HALL

▲ The mayor and the city council meet in city hall.

Big Cities in the United States

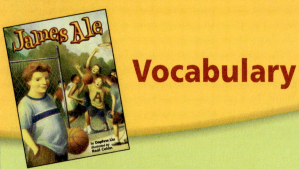

Song

The Mayor's Song

The **government** is meant to serve you.
Busy **neighborhoods** need care.
If you want a safe **community**,
Send your letters to the **mayor**!

—*Shirleyann Costigan*

Tune: "Reuben, Reuben"

Key Words

government

neighborhood

community

mayor

city council

decision

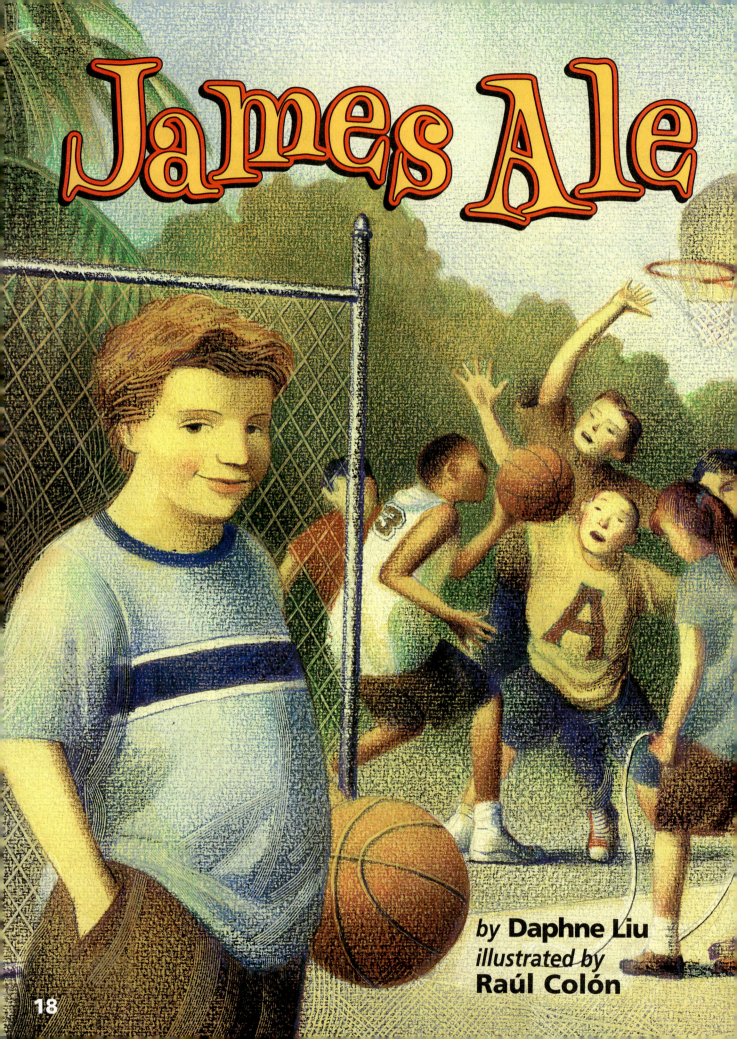

James Ale

by **Daphne Liu**

illustrated by
Raúl Colón

Read a Story

Genre

Some stories are about events that really happen. They are <mark>true stories</mark>. This one is about a real boy who changes his community.

Characters

James Ale

Mayor Kovac

Setting

This story takes place in Davie, Florida.

Davie, Florida

Selection Reading

Something happens to James' friend. What will James do?

It is another sunny day in Davie, Florida. A group of children is playing in the street, as they always do. James Ale waves to his friend. "Hey, Bobby. Catch!" he calls. Then he throws a ball high into the air.

Suddenly, a car **comes speeding** around the corner. James shouts, "Look out!" It is too late. Bobby lies on the ground. He is holding his hurt leg. A car hit Bobby!

comes speeding drives quickly

An ambulance takes Bobby away. He will be OK. James walks slowly home. He feels angry. Kids are already playing in the street again!

An ambulance A van that drives people to the hospital

"It's not fair," James thinks. "Kids shouldn't have to play in the street. Other **communities** have parks. Our **neighborhood** needs one, too!" He looks at the small **field** behind the **water plant**. "This is the perfect place for a park," James thinks. "I'm going to ask the city to build one here!"

---

field open area
water plant building where water is cleaned

Before You Move On

1. **Sequence** What happens to Bobby?
2. **Goal and Outcome** What does James want to do? Why?

James writes a **petition** for a new park. He takes his petition around to everyone in the neighborhood. Fifty kids sign it to show that they want a new park, too. Then James **makes an appointment** to talk to <mark>Mayor</mark> Kovac.

---

petition letter that asks
makes an appointment plans a time

James shows the mayor his petition. He explains why his neighborhood needs a park. He points to the place on a map where the park should be.

Mayor Kovac **is impressed**. She didn't expect a nine-year-old boy to be so organized. Still, she cannot make the <mark>decision</mark> alone. "Let me show this to the <mark>city council</mark>," she says.

James smiles and gives her a business card. It has his name and phone number. "Please call anytime," he says.

CHILDREN FOR DAVIE

JAMES ALE, Director   555-7758

◀ **business card**

---

is impressed likes what James has done

Soon James is very busy. He meets with the mayor. He writes letters to other people in the **government** and to **news reporters**. He tells everyone about the park. James **is persistent**. People begin to listen to him.

---

news reporters people who tell the news to others

is persistent keeps trying

Finally, the city council asks James to come to a city council meeting. At the meeting, Mayor Kovac **makes a wonderful announcement**: the city council has **agreed** to build a new park! Everyone cheers.

makes a wonderful announcement
tells everyone the good news
agreed decided

Today, the children in Davie have a safe place to play. It's called James Ale Park. It's one of the most popular playgrounds in Davie, Florida. The children also have a new hero, James Ale.

"I had a good idea," James says, "and I **never gave up**. It doesn't matter how old you are. If you are persistent, you can get a lot done."

---

never gave up did not stop trying

Before You Move On

1. **Character** Why is the mayor impressed with James?

2. **Sequence** James meets with Mayor Kovac twice. Then what does he do?

Meet the Illustrator

Raúl Colón

Raúl Colón can speak and read Spanish and English. He says, "You expand your mind when you know two languages. It helps your creativity."

As a child, Mr. Colón was very creative. He would draw on just about any paper he could find, even his sister's notebooks! By the time he was nine, he realized he wanted to be an illustrator. His dream came true. Now Mr. Colón illustrates books, posters, and magazines.

Think and Respond

Strategy: Sequence of Events

The events in a story happen in an order, or sequence.
To understand the sequence, look for time words.

- ✔ The words *first*, *next*, *then*, and *finally* show time order.
- ✔ Words like *suddenly*, *soon*, and *today* tell when.

Make a sequence chain for "James Ale." Show the events in
the correct order.

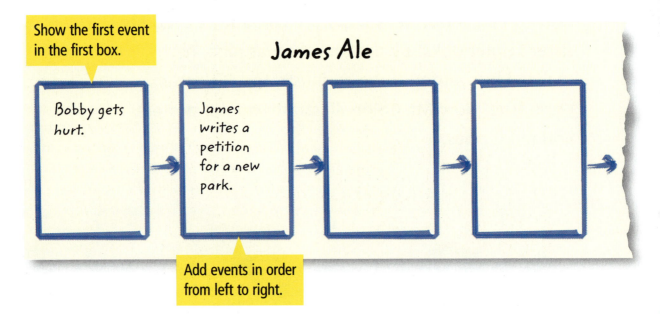

Show the first event in the first box.

James Ale

Bobby gets hurt.

James writes a petition for a new park.

Add events in order from left to right.

Interview a Character

Pretend you are James Ale. Have a partner ask you
questions about what you did to get a new park.

Talk It Over

1 **Personal Response** What would you change in your community? Why?

2 **Character** Why do you think James was successful?

3 **Prediction** One day James finds the park full of trash. What do you think he will do?

4 **Opinion** Is a park an important part of a community? Why or why not?

Compare Characters

Think of a character who made a difference in a community. How is the character like James Ale?

Content Connections

Play "Mayor, May I?"

large group

Role-play a city council meeting. Choose one person to be the mayor. Everyone takes a turn and asks the mayor for something in your community. The mayor chooses which things to do and which not to do.

Mayor, may we have a skateboard park?

ART

Make a Community Mobile

small group

What is a community? Make a mobile with your group that shows one part of a community. Then describe and explain your mobile to another group.

Community Services

Hospital

Police Department

Fire Department

Library

Community Center

Help Your Community

Internet

small group

1. Learn what kids have done in their communities.

2. Write a plan for <u>your</u> idea.

3. Go and do it! Take pictures and notes about what you do.

4. Report to your class what happened.

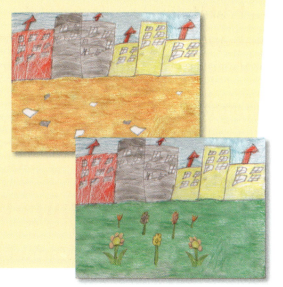

WRITING

Write a Thank-you Note

partners

Who has done something to help your community? Write to them and thank them for what they have done. Have a partner help you edit your note. Then send it.

October 12, 2004

Dear Mr. Rodriguez,
Thank you for volunteering with Big Brothers.
This helps the kids in our town.

Sincerely,
Ernesto

Draw Conclusions

When you read and **draw conclusions**, you figure out things on your own. To draw a conclusion:

✔ Read carefully.
✔ Think about the details the author gives you.
✔ Combine the details with what you already know.

Try the strategy.

At the Community Center

Many cities have community centers. Some community centers offer summer camps for children. The children can take art classes and play sports. Some centers have classes for adults, too. Adults can study to finish their high school degrees or learn English. Centers may also have things for older adults, such as hot meals, special trips, or dance lessons. People can use and enjoy the centers at any time of the year.

> I read about all the classes. Many people go to the center in my town. I can conclude that community centers are busy places.

Practice

Take this test and **draw conclusions** about "James Ale."

Read each item. Choose the best answer.

1 Look at this diagram.

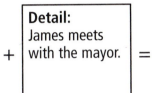

| Detail:
James takes his petition around to people in the neighborhood. | + | Detail:
James meets with the mayor. | = | Conclusion: |

Test Strategy

Read the directions carefully. The directions tell you what you need to do.

What is the best conclusion you can draw from these two details in the story?

- ⬭ James has a lot of friends.
- ⬭ James lives in a big neighborhood.
- ⬭ James is not afraid to talk to people.
- ⬭ James likes to do things out of his house.

2 **By the end of the story, what conclusion can you draw about Mayor Kovac?**

- ⬭ She likes to build parks.
- ⬭ She does not live in Davie.
- ⬭ She listens to people's ideas.
- ⬭ She is not impressed with James.

Central Park

by Ann Morris
photographs by John Paul Endress

Central Park

Central Park is a **public** park in New York City. Anyone can go there. Many people enjoy the trees and open places. It is a little bit of **nature** in an **urban** area.

public park

38

urban area

Key Words

public

nature

urban

professional

volunteer

visitor

Facts About the Park

- **Professional** builders spent 10 years making the park.

- Thousands of **volunteers** work without pay to keep the park nice.

- Twenty million **visitors** go to Central Park every year.

Read a Photo-Essay

A <mark>photo-essay</mark> is nonfiction. It uses photographs to tell about a topic.

✔ Look at all the **photos** first. See what the photo-essay is all about.

✔ Then read the words. The **captions** give details about the photos.

photo

caption

Ihsan Guitekin drives a carriage. He moved to New York City from Turkey a year and a half ago. Ihsan thinks Central Park is the best place in the city. He loves his job because he can

People go to Central Park to work. Many people have jobs in the park. One job is to drive an old-fashioned ca

Selection Reading

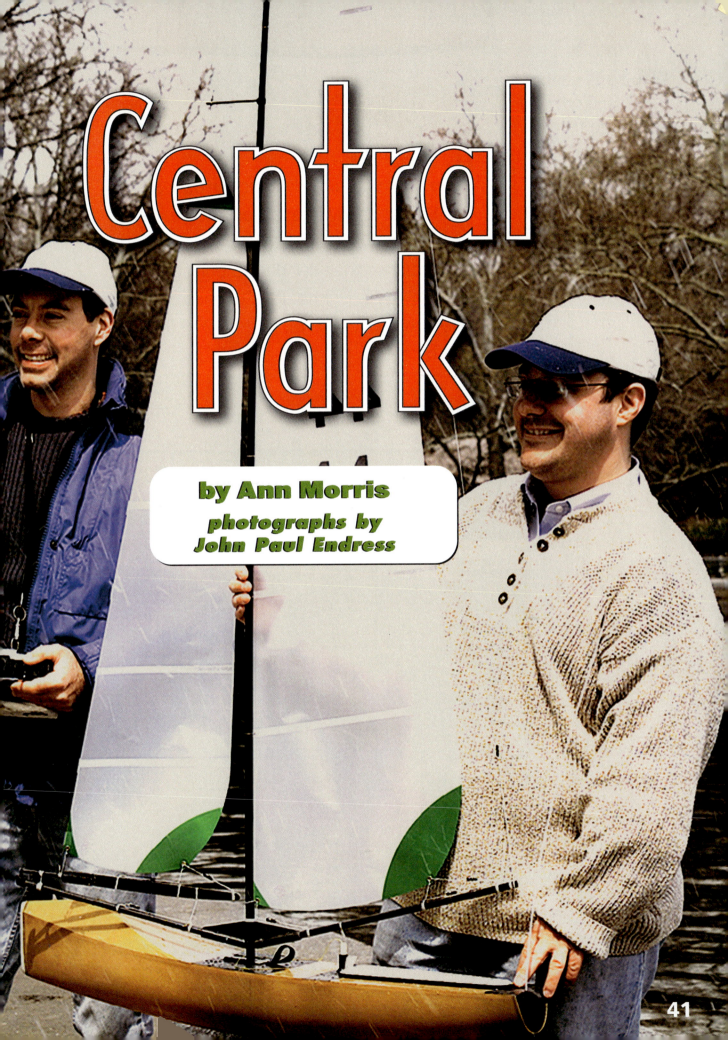

Central Park

by Ann Morris

photographs by
John Paul Endress

Set Your Purpose

Who visits Central Park? Find out why people go there.

Central Park

New York was already a big, <mark>urban</mark> area in the 1850s. Nearly one million people lived there. They wanted a place with a lot of trees and grass, so they decided to build a <mark>public</mark> park. In 1873, Central Park opened. It is a very large park with more than 270,000 trees and bushes.

Today, New York City is one of the biggest cities in the world. Central Park is very important. More **visitors** visit Central Park than any other urban park in the United States. People **get away from** the concrete sidewalks, tall buildings, and honking cars to work, play, relax, or enjoy **nature**. In fact, people go to Central Park for many different reasons.

---

get away from leave

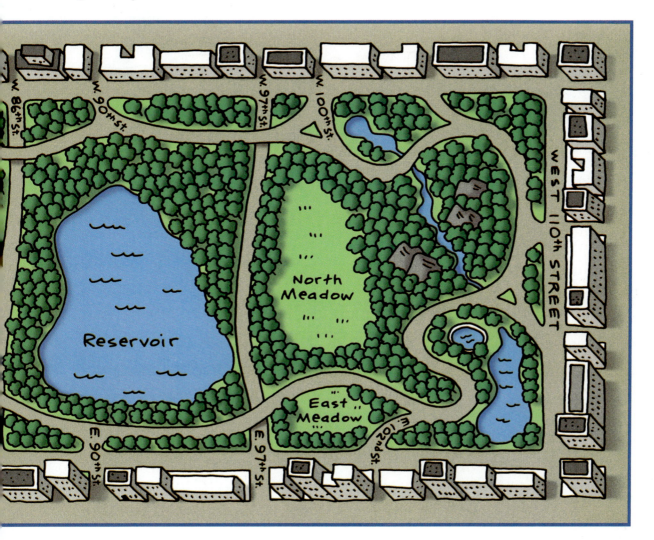

Abigail Katzen is a writer. She goes to Central Park almost every day to read, write, run, or play with her dog. She even thinks the park "is a great place to do nothing at all."

People go to Central Park to relax. Central Park has large, open areas of grass, or lawns. People sit beneath the trees and listen to the birds. After a long day of walking on concrete sidewalks, they can dig their **bare** toes into the soft grass!

bare uncovered

People go to Central Park to **exercise**. There are miles of paths through Central Park. The pathway around the outside of the park is more than six miles long. All day, bikers ride, walkers walk, and runners race up and down the busy paths.

---

exercise walk, run, bike, and play sports
trains practices
Marathon 26.2-mile running race

Antonio Medina **trains** for his high school running team in Central Park. When he moved to the United States from Mexico, he saw a woman from Mexico win the New York City **Marathon**. He says, "My goal is not just to run but to win the marathon!"

Before You Move On

1. **Details** Name two reasons people come to Central Park.

2. **Details** What is Antonio's goal?

People go to Central Park to walk their dogs. In a city full of concrete, Central Park is a wonderful place for a dog. Sometimes busy families don't have time to take their dogs there. They pay a **professional** dog-walker. These dog-walkers take dogs to the park to play and walk.

Rogerio Marlau, who is from Brazil, is a dog-walker. He takes these five dogs around the paths in the park. They love to exercise!

People go to Central Park to play. There are playgrounds to explore, a zoo to visit, and many, many statues to climb. This is the Alice in Wonderland statue. It shows characters from a famous children's book.

Ihsan Gultekin drives a carriage. He moved to New York City from Turkey a year and a half ago. Ihsan thinks Central Park is the best place in the city. He loves his job because he can practice his English all day long.

People go to Central Park to work. Many people have jobs in the park. One job is to drive **an old-fashioned carriage**. The drivers take visitors around the park and tell about the places and history of Central Park.

an old-fashioned carriage a cart with a horse like people used long ago

People go to Central Park to play music. Sometimes, professional musicians play music for thousands of people in the park. Almost every day, though, other people sit along the paths and play music for fun.

Li Si Lian plays this Chinese instrument, the erhu, in the park every weekend. Mr. Lian came from Shanghai, China, eight years ago. Mr. Lian is still learning to speak English, but the language of music is something that he can share with everyone.

Before You Move On

1. **Viewing** Do you think it is easy for Rogerio to walk all the dogs? Why or why not?

2. **Conclusion** What sounds can you hear in the park?

People go to Central Park to ice-skate. Even when the winter winds blow, it is fun to be in the park. The **ice-skating rink** is a popular place for people of all ages.

---

ice-skating rink place where people go ice-skating

Third-grader Danielle Garcia is learning to ice-skate. André Esteban Cruz is her teacher. He helps her learn how to keep her feet moving forward on the slippery ice.

These volunteers spend three hours in the park every Saturday. They work with a professional **gardener**. They feel that the park belongs to the people who live in the city.

People go to Central Park to take care of the park. The park requires a lot of work to be beautiful. **Volunteers** plant trees and flowers, fix broken bridges and buildings, rake leaves, and cut the lawns.

---

gardener person who takes care of plants

People go to Central Park to take pictures. The park is so beautiful that people love to have photos of it. Visitors take pictures of themselves in front of the statues and other **landmarks**. When they go home, they like to show these photos to their friends. Several movies have been filmed in Central Park, too.

---

landmarks places that many people know

There are many more reasons people go to Central Park. Why would you go?

Antonia Sirena was once a professional opera singer who traveled around the world. Then she became a painter. When she is in the city, she goes to Central Park every day to be outside and watch the people.

Before You Move On

1. **Details** Who takes care of the park?

2. **Paraphrase** Tell why people take pictures in Central Park.

Central Park Serenade

Beep, beep, beep,
A taxi calls.
But the traffic creeps and the traffic crawls.

Honk, honk, honk.
A bus drives by.
A startled baby starts to cry.

Clip, clop, clip, clop.
A horse trots past.
He takes his time,
    but the cars move fast.

A skater skates, and her
    wheels spin round.
A bike's brakes squeal,
    and you hear the sound.

And the pigeons coo
And the big dogs bark
And the noises echo
    through the park.

—Laura Godwin

Meet the Poet

Laura Godwin writes children's books. She lives in New York City and always hears its sounds.

Before You Move On

Main Idea What is this poem mostly about?

55

Think and Respond

Strategy: Main Idea and Details

The **main idea** is the most important idea in an article. Make a main idea diagram. Show the details that tell more about the main idea.

Write the main idea here.

People go to Central Park for many reasons.

Write details here.

to relax

Draw Conclusions

Tell why you think Central Park is so popular. Give examples from the photo-essay.

Talk It Over

1 **Personal Response** Do you want to visit Central Park? Why or why not? If you do, what do you want to see first?

2 **Comparison** How is Central Park like James Ale Park? How is it different?

3 **Opinion** Which is your favorite photograph? Why? Which is your least favorite? Why?

4 **Genre** How would "Central Park" be different if it didn't have a lot of photographs?

Compare Visuals

Compare the photographs in "Central Park" with the illustration in "Central Park Serenade."

Both the photographs and the illustration show people in Central Park.

Content Connections

Talk About Cities

partners

Look back at the photos in "Central Park." What do you like about a city? What don't you like? Tell your partner why.

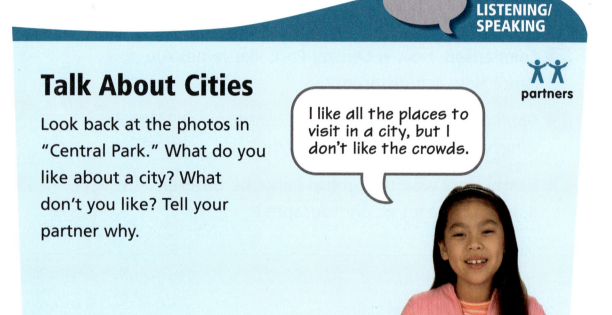

I like all the places to visit in a city, but I don't like the crowds.

2×5 MATH

Give Directions

partners

Look at the map of Central Park on pages 42 and 43. Places that are 5 inches apart on the map are one mile apart in the real park. Find two places that are one mile apart. Then give directions to your partner from one place to the other while he or she follows on the map.

Create a Brochure

1. Find your city's Web site.

2. Look for facts about the city.

3. Use the facts to make a brochure. Use maps and pictures to show what the city is like.

4. Display your brochure in the library or in another class.

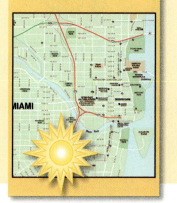

Welcome to Miami

MIAMI

WRITING

Write to Give Information

small group

Find out how your city, school, or street got its name. Then choose the best way to give information. You could write:

- a paragraph
- a poster.

Check that your writing is well-organized.

Our school was named for César E. Chávez.

Action Verbs

Listen and sing.

Song

THE MAYOR

She works, works, works
with the city council.
She speaks to us on TV.
She helps, helps, helps
everyone.
She is the mayor of
our community.

— *Jane Zion Brauer*

How Language Works

Use an **action verb** to tell what someone or something does.

To tell about one other person or thing, add **-s** to the end of the verb.

He	She	It
Examples: The boy call<u>s</u> the mayor. James call<u>s</u> the mayor. He call<u>s</u> the mayor.	Examples: The mayor like<u>s</u> the idea. Mayor Kovac like<u>s</u> the idea. She like<u>s</u> the idea.	Examples: The park change<u>s</u> the town. It change<u>s</u> the town.

Practice with a Partner

Say each sentence with the correct action verb.

want   1. Lee _____ a new park.

tell   2. He _____ his friend, Ann.

write   3. Ann _____ a letter to the mayor.

arrive   4. It _____ at the mayor's office.

read   5. The mayor _____ it to the city council.

Put It in Writing

Write about a park you know. Tell what a friend does there. When you edit your work, make sure the verbs are correct.

Mia skates on the path.

Show What You Know

Talk About Community

In this unit, you read a true story and a photo-essay. Look back at the unit. Choose your favorite picture. Write the page number on an index card. Trade cards with a partner. Talk about the pictures and why you chose them.

Make a Mind Map

Work with a partner. Make a mind map to show what you learned about communities.

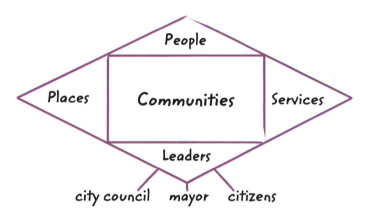

Think and Write

What did you learn about <u>your</u> community from this unit? Write sentences about it. Add this writing to your portfolio. Include work from this unit that shows what you learned about community.

Read and Learn More

Leveled Books

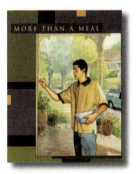

More Than a Meal
by Suzy Blackaby

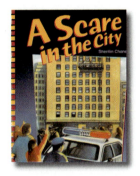

A Scare in the City
by Sherilin Chanek

Theme Library

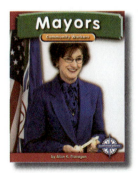

Mayors
by Alice K. Flanagan

Grandpa's Corner Store
by DyAnne DiSalvo-Ryan

Internet

Go to: www.hbavenues.com

Neighborhoods

Community

Kids' World

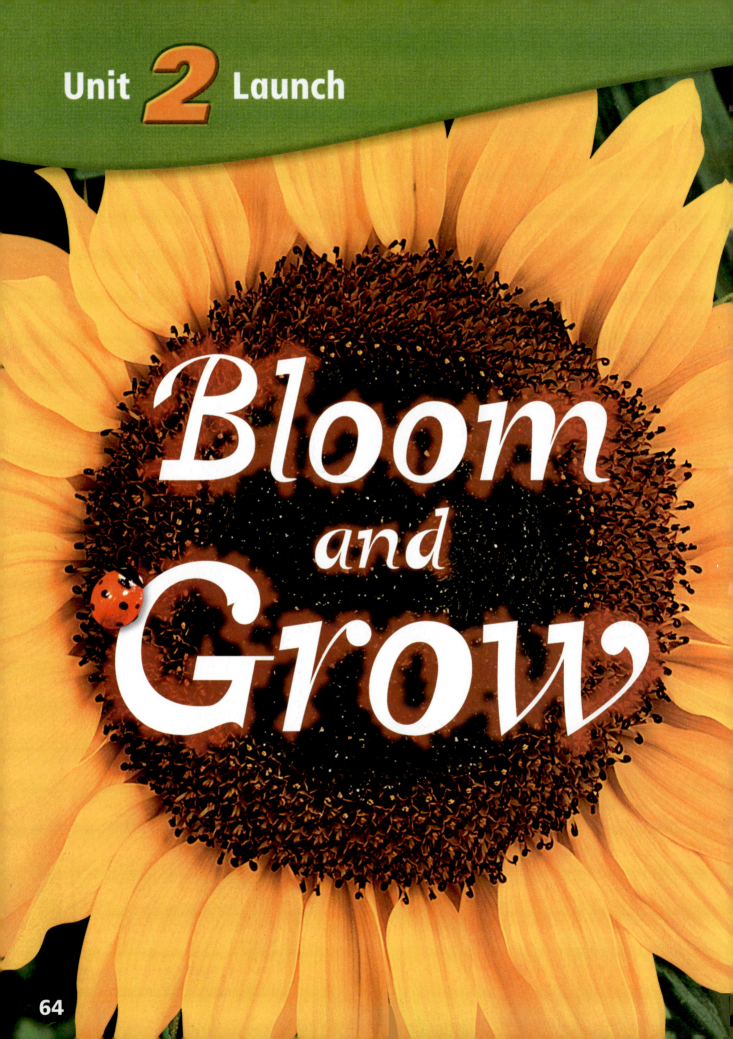

Bloom and Grow

Make a Plant Puzzle

1. Draw a plant and label its parts.
2. Cut your drawing into puzzle pieces.
3. Have a partner put the puzzle together.

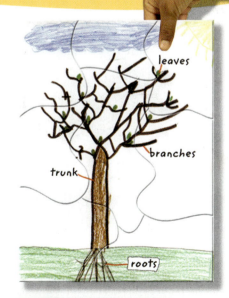

leaves

branches

trunk

roots

Parts of a Plant

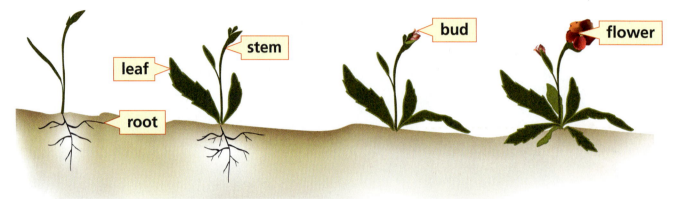

leaf

stem

bud

flower

root

The Life Cycle of a Plant

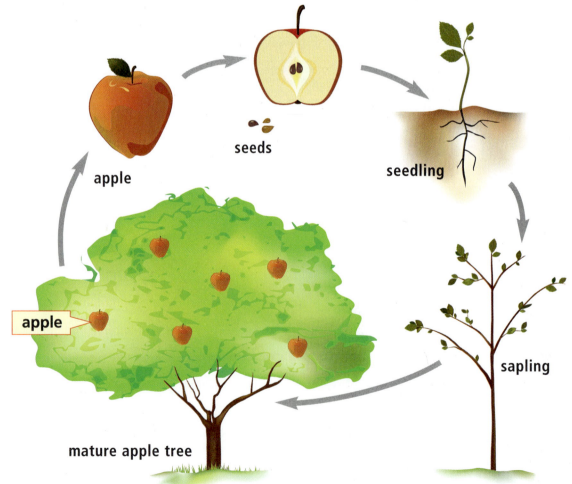

apple

seeds

seedling

apple

sapling

mature apple tree

What Plants Need

sun

soil

water

air

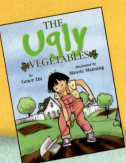

Vocabulary

THE Ugly VEGETABLES
by Grace Lin
illustrated by Maurie Manning

Song 💿

GARDEN GIFTS

Everyone is in the **garden**.
Every neighbor says hello!

How I love our **special** garden.
Everything is **beautiful**.

Tiny **seeds** grow into **flowers**.
Tender **stems** grow
    strong and green.

Ugly roots grow
    into **vegetables**
I can hardly wait to eat.

—*Maria Del Rey*

Tune: "Las mañanitas" (Morning Song)

68

Key Words

garden

special

beautiful

seed

flower

stem

ugly

vegetable

THE Ugly VEGETABLES

by
Grace Lin

illustrated by
Maurie Manning

Read a Story

Genre

This story is a <mark>personal narrative</mark>. A girl tells how she feels about her mom's garden.

Characters

a girl

her mom

Setting

This story happens in a neighborhood.

mom

neighbor

Selection Reading

71

1

What do the girl and her mom do to start their garden?

In the spring I helped my mother start our **garden**. We used tall shovels to turn the grass **upside down**, and I saw the pink worms **wriggle** around. It was hard work. When we stopped to rest, we saw that the neighbors were starting their gardens, too.

---

upside down so the dirt was on top
wriggle move

▼ worm

"Hello, Irma!" my mother called to Mrs. Crumerine. Mrs. Crumerine was digging, too. She was using a small shovel, one that fit in her hand.

"Mommy," I asked, "why are we using such big shovels? Mrs. Crumerine has a small one."

"Because our garden needs more digging," she said.

▼ shovel

73

I helped my mother plant the <mark>seeds</mark>, and we **dragged** the hose to the garden.

"Hi, Linda! Hi, Mickey!" I called to the Fitzgeralds. They were sprinkling water on their garden with green watering cans.

"Mommy," I asked, "why are we using a hose? Linda and Mickey use watering cans."

"Because our garden needs more water," she said.

---

dragged pulled

▼ hose

Then my mother drew funny pictures on pieces of paper, and I stuck them into the garden.

"Mommy," I asked, "why are we sticking these papers in the garden? Mrs. Angelhowe has seed packages in her garden."

"Because our garden is going to grow Chinese **vegetables**," she told me. "These are the names of the vegetables in Chinese, so I can tell which plants are growing where."

Before You Move On

1. **Comparison** What tools do the girl and her mom use to start a garden? What do the neighbors use?

2. **Prediction** What will Mrs. Angelhowe grow?

The plants start to grow. How are they different?

One day I saw our garden growing. Little green **stems** that looked like grass had popped out from the ground.

"Our garden's growing!" I yelled. "Our garden's growing!"

I rushed over to the neighbors' gardens to see if theirs had grown. Their plants looked like little leaves.

"Mommy," I asked, "why do our plants look like grass? The neighbors' plants look different."

"Because they are growing **flowers**," she said.

"Why can't we grow flowers?" I asked.

"These are better than flowers," she said.

▲ grass

▲ leaves

Soon all the neighbors' gardens were **blooming**. Up and down the street grew **rainbows of flowers**. The wind always smelled sweet, and butterflies and bees flew everywhere. Everyone's garden was **beautiful**, except for ours.

▲ **butterfly**

blooming full of flowers
rainbows of flowers colorful flowers

Ours was all dark green and **ugly**.

"Why didn't we grow flowers?" I asked again.

"These are better than flowers," Mommy said again.

I looked, but saw only black-purple-green vines, fuzzy wrinkled leaves, prickly stems, and a few little yellow flowers.

"I don't think so," I said.

"You wait and see," Mommy said.

vine ▶

Before long, our vegetables grew.
Some were big and lumpy. Some were
thin and green and covered with
bumps. Some were just plain **icky**
yellow. They were ugly vegetables.

icky ugly

▲ **poppy**

▲ **peony**

▲ **petunia**

Sometimes I would go over to the neighbors' and look at their pretty gardens. They would show the poppies and peonies and petunias to me, and I would feel sad that our garden wasn't as nice.

Before You Move On

1. **Details** What are the plants in the neighbors' gardens like?

2. **Character** How does the girl feel about the vegetables in the garden?

3

The girl and her mom pick the vegetables. What happens next?

One day my mother and I picked the vegetables from the garden. We filled a whole wheelbarrow full of them. We wheeled them to the kitchen. My mother washed them and took a big knife and started to **chop** them.

wheelbarrow ▶

chop cut

82

"***Aie-yow!***" she said when she cut them. She had to use all her muscles. The vegetables were hard and tough.

"This is a sheau hwang gua," Mommy said, handing me a bumpy, curled vegetable. She pointed at the other vegetables. "This is shiann tsay. That's a torng hau."

▲ **sheau hwang gua**

▲ **shiann tsay**

▲ **torng hau**

Aie-yow! Oh, no! (in Chinese)

I went outside to play. While I was playing catch with Mickey, a **magical aroma** filled the air. I saw the neighbors standing on their porches with their eyes closed, smelling the sky. They took deep breaths of air, like they were trying to eat the smell.

---

magical aroma wonderful smell

The wind carried it up and down the street. Even the bees and the butterflies seemed to smell the **scent** in the breeze.

I smelled it, too. It made me hungry, and it was coming from my house!

---

scent good smell

When I followed it to my house, my mother was putting a big bowl of soup on the table.

"This is a **special** soup," Mommy said. She gave me a small bowl full of it, and I tasted it. It was so good!

"Do you like it?" Mommy asked me.

I nodded and held out my bowl for some more.

"It's made from our vegetables," she told me.

Then the doorbell rang, and we ran to open the door.

All our neighbors were standing at the door holding flowers.

"We **noticed you were cooking**," Mr. Fitzgerald laughed as he held out his flowers. "And we thought maybe you might **be interested in a trade**!"

We laughed, too, and my mother gave them each their own bowl of her special soup.

---

noticed you were cooking could smell your food
be interested in a trade want to give us some soup if we give you some flowers

My mother told them what each vegetable was and how she grew it. She gave them the **soup recipe** and put some soup into jars for them to take home. I ate five bowls of soup.

It was the best dinner ever.

---

soup recipe directions for how to make the soup

The next spring, when my mother was starting her garden, we planted some flowers next to the Chinese vegetables. Mrs. Crumerine, the Fitzgeralds, and the Angelhowes planted some Chinese vegetables next to their flowers.

Soon the whole neighborhood was growing
Chinese vegetables in their gardens. Up and down
the street, little green plants poked out of the ground.
Some looked like leaves, and some looked like grass,
and when the flowers started blooming, you could
smell soup in the air.

Before You Move On

1. **Character** How does the girl feel about the vegetables now? Why?

2. **Details** How are the neighbors' gardens different the next spring?

How to Make **Ugly** Vegetable Soup

 1 can chicken broth

 1 cup water

 5 dried scallops

4-ounce piece of chicken

Cornstarch

 1/2 cup chopped sheau hwang gua

 1 cup chopped sy gua

 1 cup torng hau

 1 cup shiann tsay

 1 cup kong shin tsay

 pepper

Directions:

1. Heat the chicken broth, water, and scallops in a large pot.

2. Cut the chicken into bite-size pieces and roll them in cornstarch.

3. Wash all the vegetables.

4. When the broth starts to boil, put in the chicken pieces, one by one.

5. When the chicken is cooked, add the chopped sheau hwang gua and sy gua.

6. Turn the heat to low and let the soup simmer for about 10 minutes.

7. Then bring the soup to a boil.

8. Quickly add the torng hau, shiann tsay, and kong shin tsay and let them boil for 1 minute.

9. Add pepper to taste and serve!

Before You Move On

1. **Sequence** Do you add the chicken before or after the broth starts to boil?

2. **Inference** Why should you read all of the directions first?

The Ugly Vegetables

 **kong shin tsay** (kung shin zai)

 **shiann tsay** (shen zai)

jeou tsay (joe zai)

torng hau (tung how)

 **sheau hwang gua** (show hwang gwa)

sy gua (see gwa)

 kuu gua (coo gwa)

fwo loo fwo (foo loo foo)

Meet the Author

Grace Lin

Grace Lin's mother really had a vegetable garden. "My mom had her own ideas about what to grow in a garden," she says, "But I wanted my mom's garden to look pretty like other gardens on our block." That is how *The Ugly Vegetables* story began.

Ms. Lin says, "When kids read my stories, they can see themselves or their friends. They learn a little bit about Chinese culture, too."

AWARD WINNER

Think and Respond

Strategy: Make Comparisons

To make comparisons, look for how people and things:

- ✔ are alike
- ✔ are different.

Compare the gardeners in "The Ugly Vegetables."
Make a Venn diagram.

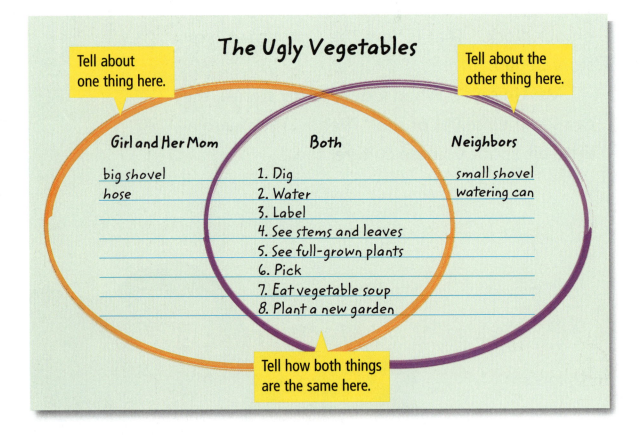

The Ugly Vegetables

Tell about one thing here.

Tell about the other thing here.

Girl and Her Mom

big shovel
hose

Both

1. Dig
2. Water
3. Label
4. See stems and leaves
5. See full-grown plants
6. Pick
7. Eat vegetable soup
8. Plant a new garden

Neighbors

small shovel
watering can

Tell how both things are the same here.

Retell the Story

Retell the story to a partner. Does your retelling match your partner's? What was different? Talk about it.

Talk It Over

1 **Personal Response** If you had a garden, what would you plant? Why?

2 **Conclusion** How did the neighborhood change because of the ugly vegetables?

3 **Speculate** Imagine that some new neighbors start a vegetable garden. What would the girl say to them?

4 **Point of View** Would "The Ugly Vegetables" be different if the girl's neighbors told the story? How?

Compare Genres

Compare the story and the recipe. How are they different? How are they the same?

Content Connections

Tell a Story

small group

In the story, the girl learned about flowers and her neighbors learned about Chinese vegetables. The neighborhood changed because people shared and learned new ideas. With your group, talk about a time you learned something new. How did it change you?

ART

Design a Shoebox Garden

Internet

on your own

Plan your own garden. Find and label pictures of plants and flowers you would like to grow. Glue the pictures in a shoebox. Then ask and answer questions about your "garden."

Community Garden

Tulips

Bluebonnets

Eggplant

Make a Class Graph

large group

1. Ask five people, "What is your least favorite vegetable?" Write the answer.

2. Share the results with your class. Then make a class graph.

3. Talk about the graph. What do the results tell you?

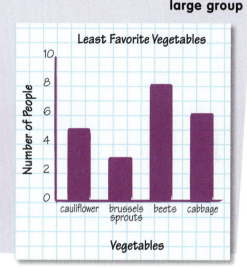

Least Favorite Vegetables

Number of People / Vegetables
cauliflower, brussels sprouts, beets, cabbage

WRITING

Write a Recipe

on your own

Who is the best cook in your family? Ask the cook how to make your family's favorite soup. Write the directions. Add your recipe to a class cookbook. Talk about the different recipes.

Black Bean Soup

Every Sunday my family has black bean soup. How do you make it? My grandmother told me.

Ingredients:

1 large ham hock
3 quarts water
1 pound dried black beans
1 red onion, chopped

1 bay leaf
32-ounce can of whole
    tomatoes with juice
3/4 teaspoon salt
1 tablespoon lime juice

Directions:

1. Cook ham hock in water for one hour.

99

Identify Supporting Details

Supporting details tell more about a main idea. To identify supporting details:

✔ Read carefully.
✔ Think about the main idea.
✔ Look for details that tell more about the main idea.

Try the strategy for Part **1** of "The Ugly Vegetables."

from **THE Ugly VEGETABLES**

In the spring I helped my mother start our garden. We used tall shovels to turn the grass upside down, and I saw the pink worms wriggle around. It was hard work. When we stopped to rest, we saw that the neighbors were starting their gardens, too.

The main idea in the first part is that the girl helped her mother start a garden. One detail is that they used tall shovels.

Practice

Take this test and <mark>identify supporting details</mark> in "The Ugly Vegetables."

Read each item. Choose the best answer.

1 **Look at the diagram.**

Main Idea
Everyone's garden was beautiful, except for ours.

Detail: Up and down the street grew rainbows of flowers.	Detail: Ours was all dark green and ugly.	Detail:

Which of these details best supports the main idea?

- ⬭ Our vegetables were big and lumpy.
- ⬭ Our neighbors grew Chinese vegetables.
- ⬭ Our garden needed more digging and more water.
- ⬭ Our garden had labels Mom drew on pieces of paper.

> ✓ **Test Strategy**
>
> Look for key words like *best* and *not*. They will help you find the correct answer.

2 **Which detail does *not* support this main idea?**
Main Idea: **Everyone liked the special soup.**

- ⬭ I ate five bowls of soup.
- ⬭ The neighbors took home soup in jars.
- ⬭ My mother told them what each vegetable was.
- ⬭ The whole neighborhood planted Chinese vegetables next year.

Plants Alive!

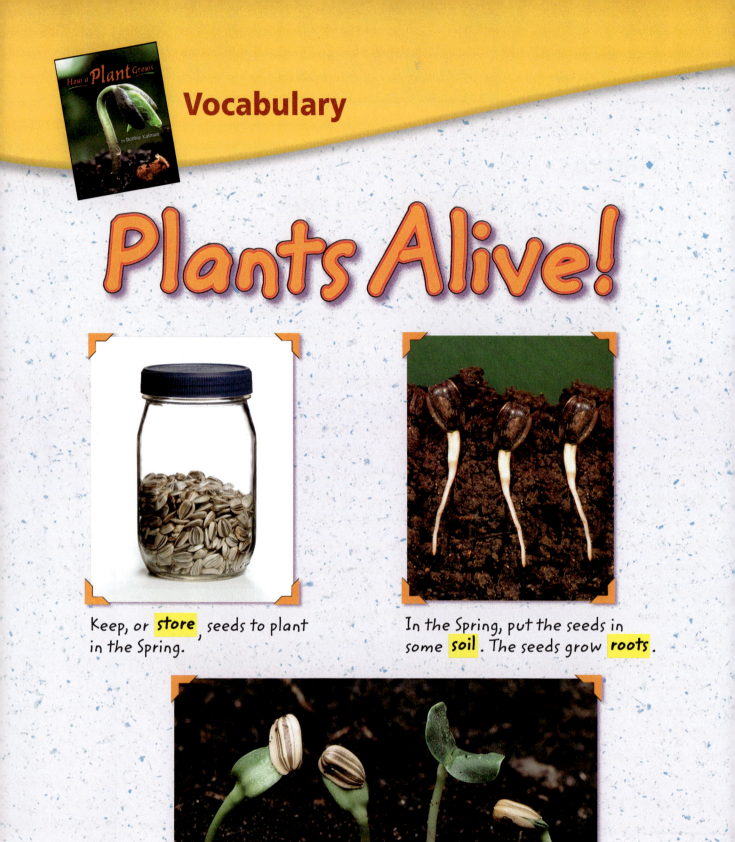

Keep, or **store**, seeds to plant in the Spring.

In the Spring, put the seeds in some **soil**. The seeds grow **roots**.

Soon, you'll have **seedlings**. Growing plants is a simple **process**.

Did You Know?

✓ **Minerals** are in the soil. A plant uses minerals for food.

✓ A plant has a **life cycle**. That means plants go through the same steps as they grow.

Key Words

seedling

process

life cycle

soil

mineral

root

store

Life Cycle of a Sunflower

seeds

sprout

seedling

plant with flowers

seeds from the flowers

Read a Science Article

A <mark>science article</mark> is nonfiction. It can tell how something in nature works.

✔ Look for **section headings**. They tell you what each part of the article is about.

section heading

The Life of a Seed Plant

These pictures show how a bean plant grows from a seed. Some plants, such as beans, take less than one year to go through these stages, or <mark>life cycle</mark>, before they die. Other plants take two or more years to complete their life cycles.

✔ Study the **diagrams** and **captions** to find more facts about the topic.

 Selection Reading

How a Plant Grows

by Bobbie Kalman

What Are Plants?

Plants are living things. They are the only living things that can make their own food. Plants cannot move from place to place as animals can. They stay in the same **spot** their whole life. Plants live in <mark>soil</mark>, sand, and rock. Some even grow on top of other plants!

---

spot place

Plants grow on top of a fallen tree. ▶

WHERE PLANTS GROW

soil

sand

rock

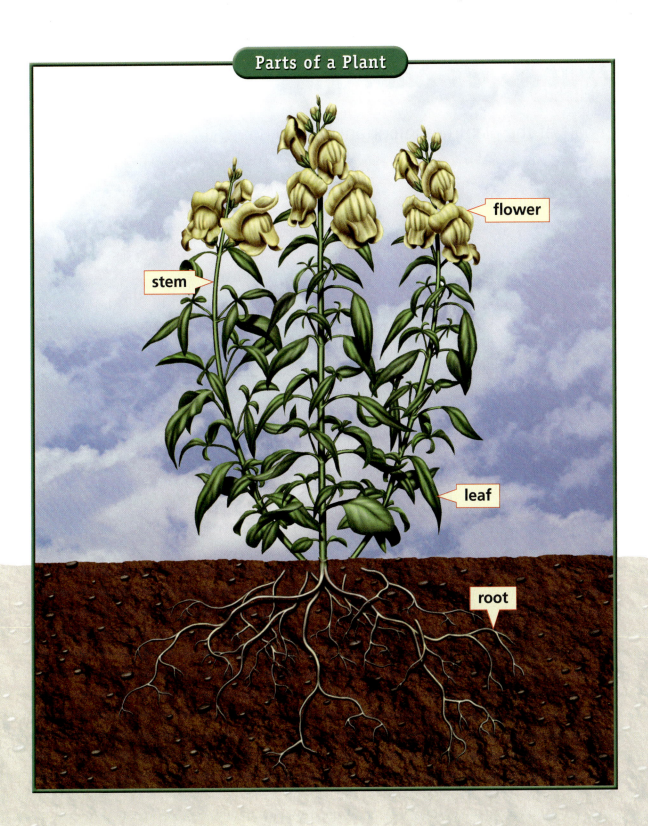

flower

stem

leaf

root

Most plants have **roots**, leaves, flowers, and a stem. Many grow from seeds.

Before You Move On
1. **Inference** What is one way that plants are different from people?
2. **Details** Name four parts of a plant.

107

What Does Each Part Do?

Each part of the plant has important jobs to do.

Leaves catch sunlight and use it to make food for the plant.

The stem carries water and **minerals** from the roots to the leaves. Food made in the leaves travels down the stem to the roots.

Roots **absorb** water and minerals from the soil for the plant to use. Roots also **store** extra food.

---

absorb take in

Not all leaves are wide and flat. The needles on cactus plants and evergreen trees are thin, waxy leaves.

Evergreen Tree

needle

Prickly Pear Cactus

needle

Some vegetables, such as carrots, radishes, and beets, are roots. They store food for the plant to use over the winter. They also give the plant energy to grow a new stem and leaves in the spring.

These carrots are roots. ▶

Before You Move On

1. **Details** Tell two jobs that roots have.
2. **Inference** What can happen to a plant if the leaves die? Why?

The Life of a Seed Plant

These pictures show how a bean plant grows from a seed. Some plants, such as beans, take less than one year to go through these stages, or **life cycle**, before they die. Other plants take two or more years to complete their life cycles.

Life Cycle of a Bean Plant

insect

flower

stem

leaf

stem

seed

root

soil

1. The seed breaks open. A root grows down into the soil, and a stem grows upward. This **process** is called germination.

2. The small young plant, or **seedling**, grows leaves and can make its own food.

3. When the plant is fully grown, it makes flowers. Insects or birds visit the flowers.

fruit

seed

4. The insects or birds bring parts of other flowers, called pollen, with them. The parts of the two flowers mix. This process is called pollination. The plant can now make seeds.

5. Parts of the flower die and a fruit grows inside of it. Seeds grow inside the fruit.

6. The seeds fall from the plant so they have room to grow. They become new plants.

Before You Move On

1. **Paraphrase** Tell what happens during germination.

2. **Sequence** Put these in the correct order: fruit, flower, seedling.

Seeds on the Move

Once seeds are made, they need places to grow. Animals, wind, and water help move the seeds of plants.

Some seeds are covered in tiny hooks that catch on animal fur. An animal carries the seed with it until the hooks break. The seeds then drop and become new plants.

This duck carries seeds on its feathers.

Seeds can also be carried by wind or water. Maple seeds, for example, have wings and fly like small helicopters.

Dandelion seeds have parachutes to **float away** on a breeze.

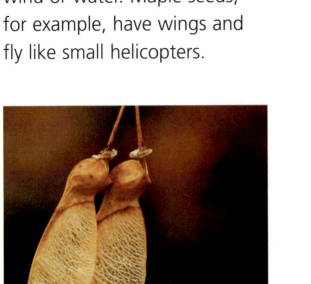

▲ maple seed

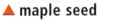

▲ helicopter

▲ dandelion seed

▲ parachute

▲ coconut

Some seeds, such as coconuts, float on water and sail to their new homes. Wherever the seed lands, it grows roots and becomes a new plant.

---

float away fly away

Before You Move On

1. **Main Idea and Details** Tell how some seeds move.
2. **Viewing** How does the photograph on page 112 help you understand how seeds move?

Why Plants Are Important

People and other creatures cannot live without plants. Take a look at your lunch. How many things are made of plants? Could you live without eating plants?

Plants in the Food We Eat

peanuts + grapes + wheat → peanut butter and jelly sandwich

apples → apple sauce

bananas → banana

People use plants for food, but they also need them for other things. Medicine, clothes, and furniture are made from plants. Look around you. What else do you see that is made from a plant?

Things Made from Plants

cotton plant

shirt

jeans

pine tree

chair

table

Before You Move On
1. **Personal Experience** What other foods come from plants?
2. **Conclusion** Why are plants important?

Think and Respond

Strategy: Identify Supporting Details

An article can have several main, or important, ideas. Here is one main idea from page 106.

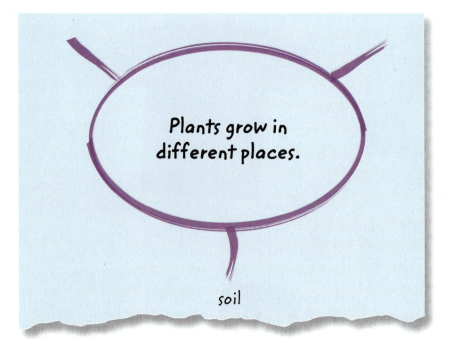

Plants grow in different places.

soil

Now make a cluster for each of the main ideas in this science article. Add supporting details to each cluster.

✔ Each part of a plant has a special job.
✔ Plants have a life cycle.
✔ Seeds move in different ways.
✔ Plants are important for many reasons.

Give Information

Work in a group of five. Each person chooses one main idea. Use the cluster and the pictures from the selection to give information about the main idea.

Talk It Over

1 **Personal Response** What is the most interesting fact you learned about plants?

2 **Conclusion** How do stems and roots help a plant grow?

3 **Steps in a Process** Explain the life cycle of a plant.

4 **Inference** Why do you think most people like plants?

Compare Topics

Compare what you learned about plants in "The Ugly Vegetables" and "How a Plant Grows."

The story told us how to grow plants, but the article told us how plants make seeds.

Content Connections

LISTENING/
SPEAKING

Guess the Plant

small group

Find something made from a plant. Have your group ask questions until they guess your object. Take turns. Then display all the objects. Tell the plant each object comes from. Describe your displays to the class.

SOCIAL
STUDIES

Make a Product Map

on your own

1. Visit the grocery store. Look at the labels on the fruits and vegetables.

2. Draw and label pictures for two fruits and two vegetables. Write the state or country where the foods are grown.

3. Put your pictures on a map. Use yarn to connect each place to where you live.

4. Tell the class how the food gets to your city or town.

UNITED STATES

El Paso

Grapes

MEXICO

Watch the Sprouts

partners

Soak lentils in a bowl of water overnight. Then put them in a jar. Turn the lid tightly. Place the jar on its side. What do you think will happen over the next two weeks? Make an observation log. Compare your results with a partner.

WRITING

Write to Give Information

on your own

Internet

What's your favorite plant? Find out how to grow it. Choose the best form to tell about it:

- a paragraph
- directions.

Be sure to give important details about the plant. Check that your writing makes sense and is clear.

> To grow pansies, find a sunny or partly shady spot. You can plant the seeds in the spring when the ground is soft.

The Verbs *have* and *be*

Listen and chant.

Chant

My Plant

My plant is big.

My plant is tall.

My plant is the nicest plant of all.

It has long roots

And a big strong stem.

It has pretty flowers.

Just look at them!

—*Jane Zion Brauer*

How Language Works

Some **verbs** do not show action.

The Verb *have*	The Verb *be*
■ Do you want to tell what someone or something has? Then use the verb **has** or **have**. Examples: I **have** a garden. Dan **has** a garden. We **have** a lot of plants.	■ Do you want to tell what someone or something is or is like? Then use the verb **am**, **is**, or **are**. Examples: I **am** a gardener. Mia **is** a gardener. We **are** good gardeners.

Practice with a Partner

Choose the correct red verb. Then say the sentence.

is / are **1.** The garden _____ pretty.

is / are **2.** The flowers _____ yellow and red.

has / have **3.** I _____ a garden hose.

am / is **4.** I _____ ready to water the plants.

has / have **5.** Oh, no! The hose _____ a hole in it!

Put It in Writing

Draw a garden of your own. Write about the flowers or vegetables. When you edit your work, make sure the verbs are correct.

My garden is big. It has red flowers.

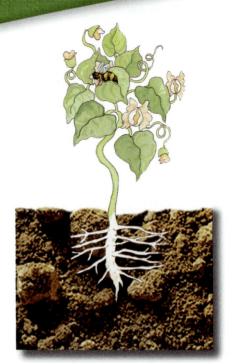

Show What You Know

Talk About Plants

In this unit, you read a story and a science article about plants. Look back at this unit. Find your favorite plant fact. Tell your group about the fact and why you think it is interesting.

Make a Mind Map

Work with a partner. Make a mind map to show what you learned about plants.

Uses of plants

Plant life cycle

How seeds move

Plants

stems

Parts of a plant

Where plants live

leaves

roots

Think and Write

Think about why plants are important to you. Write a paragraph. Add this writing to your portfolio. Include work from this unit about plants.

Read and Learn More

Leveled Books

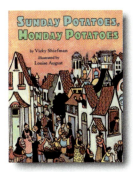

**Sunday Potatoes,
Monday Potatoes**
by Vicky Shiefman

**What's Best
For Red?**
by Casey Eggers

Theme Library

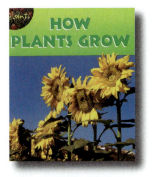

How Plants Grow
by Angela Royston

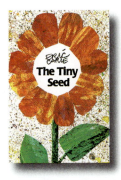

The Tiny Seed
by Eric Carle

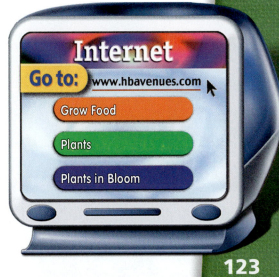

Internet
Go to: www.hbavenues.com
Grow Food
Plants
Plants in Bloom

MOON LIGHT, MOON BRIGHT

Make the Phases of the Moon

1. Stand in a circle around a ball. One student shines a light on the ball.
2. Which part of the ball is bright? Draw it.
3. Compare drawings with a partner. How does the "Moon" look in your drawing?
4. Tell a partner what phase your drawing shows.

full moon   **quarter moon**   **crescent moon**

Moon Phases

| new | waxing crescent | first quarter | waxing gibbous | full | waning gibbous | last quarter | waning crescent |

The Moon's Orbit

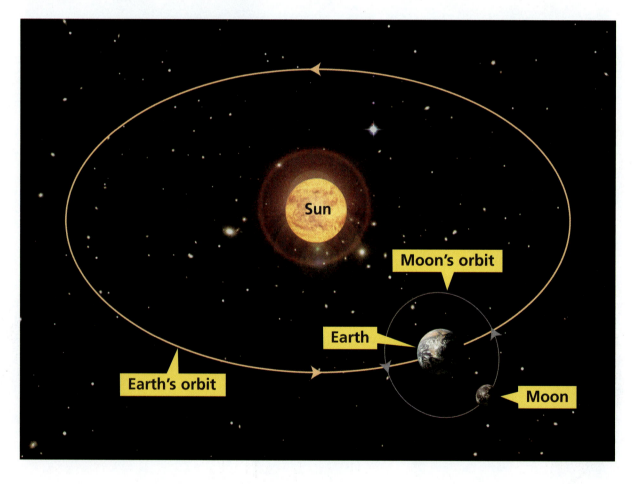

The Solar System

Neptune
Saturn
Mars
Venus
Pluto
Uranus
Earth
Mercury
Jupiter
SUN

▲ This diagram compares sizes of the planets, but it does not show distance.

Space Travel

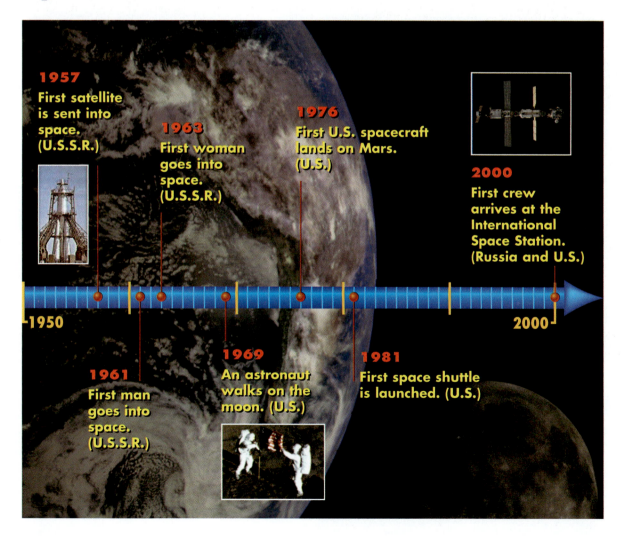

1957
First satellite is sent into space. (U.S.S.R.)

1963
First woman goes into space. (U.S.S.R.)

1976
First U.S. spacecraft lands on Mars. (U.S.)

2000
First crew arrives at the International Space Station. (Russia and U.S.)

1950

2000

1961
First man goes into space. (U.S.S.R.)

1969
An astronaut walks on the moon. (U.S.)

1981
First space shuttle is launched. (U.S.)

Moon Talk

What do people see in the Moon? People have different **ideas**. Some see hands in a full moon. Others see a rabbit in the Moon. My friend tried to **convince** me that there is a frog in the Moon. All I see is a man's face!

IN INDIA

IN MEXICO

IN CHINA

IN THE U.S.

Key Words
idea
convince
impossible
stretch
reach
plan
wish for
dream

It used to be **impossible** to get to the Moon. You could **stretch** and stretch, but you could not **reach** it.

Our country wanted to go to the Moon. Some people made a **plan** and built a spaceship. It landed on the Moon in 1969.

Today, you can **wish for** a trip to the Moon, and your **dream** may come true.

The Fox in the Moon

Based on a Peruvian Folk Tale

retold by Juan Quintana and Michael Ryall

illustrated by Francisco X. Mora

Read a Folk Tale

Genre

A **folk tale** is an old story that tells why something is the way it is. This one tells why some people see a fox when they look at the full moon.

Characters

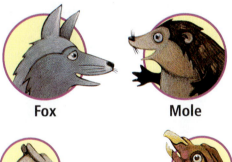

Fox

Mole

Llama

Condor

Bear

Setting

The folk tale happens at night in the mountains of Peru.

Peru

▲ mountains of Peru

Selection Reading

Fox and Mole are friends. Find out where they want to go.

A long, long time ago, when animals could still talk, Fox and Mole were the best of friends. On full-moon nights, they both liked to sit outside in the **moonlight**. They would often stay up late into the night telling stories and **sharing dreams**.

---

moonlight light that shines from the Moon
sharing dreams talking about their dreams

One night, Fox told Mole his craziest dream of all: he wanted to go to the Moon.

Mole didn't care one bit about going to the Moon. All he cared about was eating **worms**—big, fat, **juicy** worms. He dreamed about having worms for breakfast, lunch, and dinner. Worms were the first thing he thought about when he woke up and the last thing he thought about before going to sleep.

---

worms small animals that live under the ground
juicy wet

"Mole," asked Fox, "what do you **wish for**?"

"Worms!" said Mole. "I wish I had worms to eat all day long! What about you?"

"I wish I could go to the Moon," said Fox. "Hey! I've got an **idea**. Will you come with me, Mole?"

"It's so high," Mole said. "It's **impossible**."

"But I have a **plan**," said Fox. "We'll wait for the crescent moon. Then we can tie a very long rope to the Moon and climb up the rope—it will be easy!"

Mole just **frowned**.

"There are worms on the Moon," Fox said.

Mole's eyes became big and round. "Worms?"

"Yes! You can have worms for breakfast, lunch, and dinner if you want."

"And **dessert**, too?" asked Mole.

"Sure," Fox answered.

And so Fox <mark>**convinced**</mark> Mole to go with him to the Moon.

---

frowned had a sad look on his face
dessert the sweet food after lunch or dinner

Before You Move On

1. **Goal** What does Fox want to do?

2. **Inference** What does Mole think of Fox's plan?

2

Fox and Mole make a rope. How do they tie it to the Moon?

he next night, they started making the longest rope in the world.

They worked together
night...   after night...   after night...

until they finished the rope. Then, they waited for the crescent moon to **appear**.

Finally the Moon was just the right shape.

---

appear show in the sky

ox and Mole went to see Bear in his **cave**.

"Dear Bear," they said, "you are the best tree-climber of all. Please, oh please, climb to the top of the highest tree and tie this rope around the Moon."

Bear said he would try.

Bear climbed up, up, and up to the top of the highest tree. When he got to the top, he stood on **tip-toe** and stretched as far as he could. But he couldn't reach the Moon. It was too high.

---

cave   home inside the mountain
tip-toe   the ends of his toes

So, Fox and Mole asked Llama for help.

"Dear Llama, you are the best mountain-climber of all. Please, oh please, climb to the top of the highest mountain and tie this rope around the Moon."

Llama said she would try.

Llama climbed up, up, and up to the top of the highest mountain. When she got to the top, she s-t-r-e-t-c-h-e-d her neck as far as she could. But she couldn't reach the Moon. It was too high.

So, Fox and Mole asked Condor for help.

"Dear Condor, you can fly higher than anybody else. Please, oh please, fly as high as you can and tie this rope around the Moon."

Condor said he would try.

Condor grabbed the rope with his **beak** and flew
high into the sky. Up, up, and up he flew in great big
circles, each circle higher than the last. When he flew
as high as he could, he s-t-r-e-t-c-h-e-d his neck
and—at last!—he tied the rope around the Moon.

Before You Move On

1. **Details** What does
   Bear climb? What does
   Llama climb?

2. **Inference** Why can
   Condor reach farther
   than Bear or Llama?

beak mouth

141

3

Do you think
Fox and Mole
will get to
the Moon?

"ooray!" shouted Mole.

"Thank you, Condor!" shouted Fox. He tied the other end of the rope to a tree and **immediately** started to climb.

"Come on, Mole," Fox yelled. "It's Moon time!"

---

immediately right away

Mole watched Fox climb the rope. The Moon was
so high! He closed his eyes and thought about all the
worms on the Moon. Then he opened his eyes and very
slowly, very carefully, he started to climb up the rope.

Up, up, and up they climbed, higher than the
highest trees.

" h, I get scared when I look down! Hey, Fox," shouted Mole. "Are we almost there?"

"Just a little bit higher, Mole," replied Fox. "Think of the worms. And don't look down whatever you do!"

Up, up, and up they climbed, higher than the highest mountains.

"Hey, Fox," shouted Mole again. "Are we almost there? It's cold up here, and I get **dizzy** every time I look down."

"We're almost there, Mole!" shouted Fox. "Just keep thinking about the worms. And remember, don't look down!"

---

dizzy a feeling that my head is spinning

p, up, and up they climbed, higher than the highest cloud. Then Mole looked down.

He got so dizzy that he let go of the rope and fell down,

down,

down

to the ground.

He hit the Earth so hard that he went deep into the ground. Mole was **very embarrassed** and wanted to hide. That's why Mole still lives **underground** to this day.

---

very embarrassed not proud of himself
underground in a hole in the ground

And Fox? Fox climbed all the way to the Moon and lived there happily for the rest of his life. And in Peru, where this story comes from, people say that on a clear night you can see the shape of a fox in the Moon.

Before You Move On

1. **Outcome/Character** Did Fox's dream come true? How do you think he feels?

2. **Outcome** Did Mole reach his goal? Why?

Meet the Illustrator

Francisco X. Mora

Francisco X. Mora grew up in Mexico. He started studying English in first grade. He really began to speak English when he moved to the United States about 20 years ago. He says he is still learning things about English.

Mr. Mora says, "When I found the language of art, I knew I could be speaking forever." He encourages his young friends to speak two languages so they have a wide range of opportunities.

Think and Respond

Strategy: Goal and Outcome

Some stories, like "The Fox in the Moon," tell how a character reaches a goal. In these stories, look for the:

- ✔ goal
- ✔ events
- ✔ outcome.

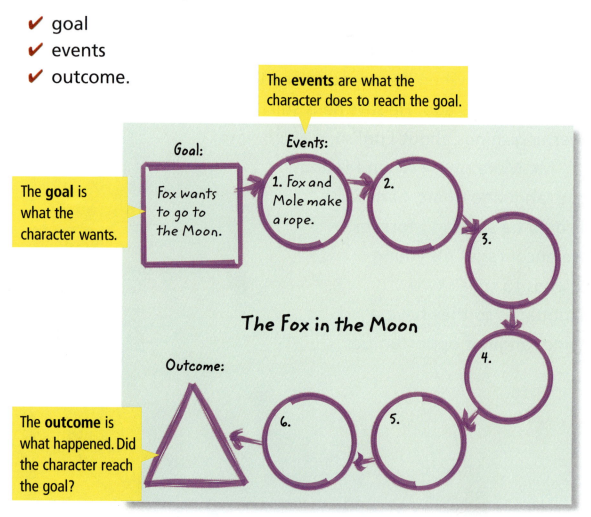

The **events** are what the character does to reach the goal.

Goal:

The **goal** is what the character wants.

Fox wants to go to the Moon.

Events:

1. Fox and Mole make a rope.

2.

3.

4.

5.

6.

The Fox in the Moon

Outcome:

The **outcome** is what happened. Did the character reach the goal?

Make a story map for "The Fox in the Moon."
Show Fox's goal, the events, and the outcome.

Retell the Story

Retell the folk tale to a partner. Does your retelling match your partner's? What was different? Talk about it.

Talk It Over

1. **Personal Response** Which part of the story did you like best? What questions do you have?

2. **Judgment** Was Fox's plan good? Why or why not?

3. **Opinion** Do you think Fox was a good friend to Mole? Explain. Give examples from the story.

4. **Fantasy** A folk tale can include fantasy, or things that could never happen. Tell two things in this folk tale that are fantasy.

Compare Folk Tales

What folk tales have you read or heard at home? Are any of them like "The Fox in the Moon"? How?

Content Connections

Change the Setting

partners

What if this folk tale happened in your city? What kind of animals live there? How could they reach the Moon? Draw a storyboard. Use it to tell your new story.

SOCIAL
STUDIES

Compare Folk Tales

small group

People in Peru see a fox in the Moon. What do people in other cultures see when they look at the Moon? Read more stories. Then make a chart to compare them. What can you say about how people have <u>different</u> ideas about the <u>same</u> thing?

Country	Who	How They Got in the Moon
Peru	fox	climbed a rope

Research the Solar System

Internet

Find out about a place in our solar system. Then make a card for a fact file. Tell your group about the place, and have your group ask questions about it.

Saturn

Saturn has more rings than any other planet.

Write a Dream Statement

Fox had a dream: he wanted to go to the Moon. What is your dream? How will you do it? Write about your dream. Draw a picture to show what you want to do or be.

My dream is to be the world's youngest astronaut. I will study hard. I will learn all about space.

Summarize

A <mark>summary</mark> tells the important information in what you read. To summarize:

✔ Tell the main ideas.
✔ Don't repeat any information.
✔ Keep your summary short.

Try the strategy. First make a list of the main ideas in Part **1** of "The Fox in the Moon." Then summarize them.

from The Fox in the Moon

"There are worms on the Moon," Fox said.

Mole's eyes became big and round. "Worms?"

"Yes! You can have worms for breakfast, lunch, and dinner if you want."

"And dessert, too?" asked Mole.

"Sure," Fox answered.

And so Fox convinced Mole to go with him to the Moon.

Fox's dream is to go to the Moon. Mole wants to eat worms. Fox tells Mole there are worms on the Moon and convinces Mole to go with him to the Moon.

Practice

Take this test and **summarize** "The Fox in the Moon."

Read each item. Choose the best answer.

1 Read Part **2** on pages 136–141 again. Which of these sentences belongs in a summary of Part **2**?

✓ **Test Strategy**

Read all of the answer choices before you choose an answer.

- ⬭ Bear lived in a cave.
- ⬭ Fox told Mole his dream.
- ⬭ Fox and Mole made a long rope.
- ⬭ The Moon was not the right shape.

2 Which of the following completes this summary of the whole story?

> Fox convinced Mole to go to the Moon. They made a rope and asked their friends for help.
>
> _____
>
> _____

- ⬭ Fox and Mole climbed up the rope. Mole asked, "Are we there yet?" Fox told Mole not to look down.

- ⬭ Fox and Mole asked Bear, Llama, and Condor for help. Condor tied the rope to the Moon.

- ⬭ Fox and Mole climbed the rope. Mole fell. Fox climbed to the Moon. You can still see a fox in the Moon.

- ⬭ Fox and Mole climbed the rope. Mole was scared. He got dizzy and fell down. Mole was embarrassed.

Song

ON THE MOON

Mountains, craters. Mountains, craters.
On the Moon. On the Moon.
Find them on the surface.
Find them on the surface.
Look and see. Look and see.

—*Sheron Long*

meteorite

crater

Tune: "Frère Jacques"

156

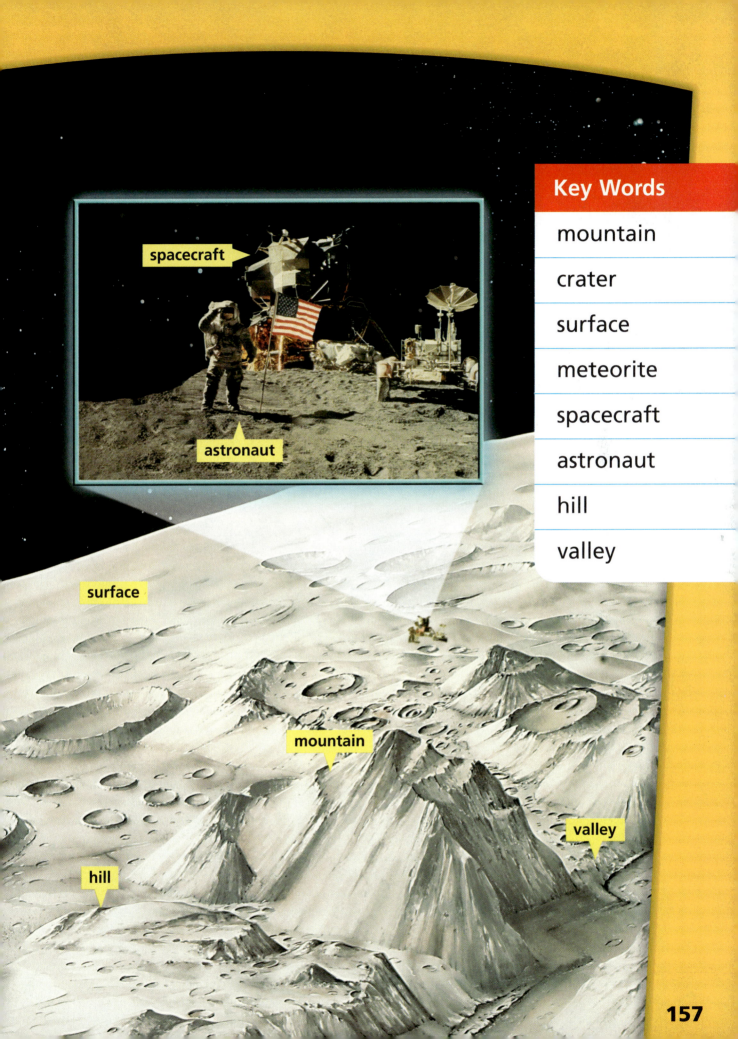

spacecraft

astronaut

surface

mountain

valley

hill

Key Words

mountain

crater

surface

meteorite

spacecraft

astronaut

hill

valley

157

Read a Science Article

A **science article** is nonfiction. It gives facts about a topic.

✔ Look for **maps**. They show you where things are.

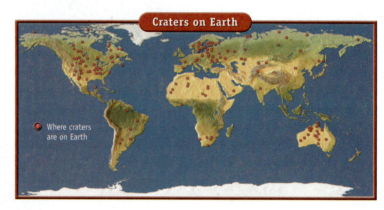

Craters on Earth

Where craters are on Earth

✔ Read **section headings**, **captions**, and **diagrams** to find facts.

 Selection Reading

The MOON

by Janine Wheeler

What Is on the Moon?

When you look at the Moon, you see light and dark spots. Did you ever wonder what they are?

Light The light that you can see is from the Sun. The Sun shines on the Moon just as it shines on the Earth. The sunlight makes the Moon bright enough for us to see it here on Earth. The sunlight also shows the dark and light places on the **surface** of the Moon.

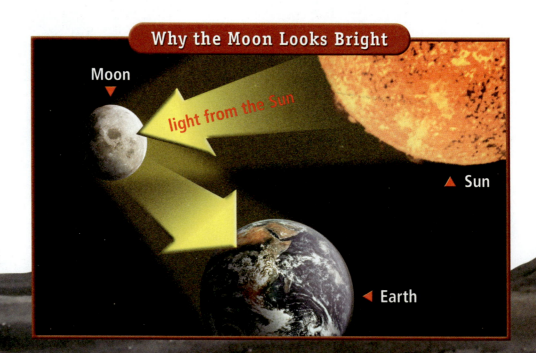

Why the Moon Looks Bright

Moon

light from the Sun

▲ Sun

◀ Earth

Mountains and Hills The brighter and taller places are mostly **mountains** and **hills**. Just like on Earth, there are mountain ranges on the Moon. Some Moon mountains reach up to 25,000 feet high.

▼ **This Moon mountain is more than 13,000 feet high.**

Valleys The darker places you see on the Moon are low areas. Low areas between two mountains are called **valleys**. The valleys are smooth and flat, like the inside of a **crater**. In fact, some of them are craters.

A mountain on the Moon
▼

A valley on the Moon
▼

Before You Move On
1. **Graphic Aids** What makes the Moon bright?
2. **Details** What is a Moon valley like?

Craters There are thousands of craters on the surface of the Moon. Rocks fly through space all the time. When they hit the surface of the Moon, they are called **meteorites** . Meteorites make dents, called craters. Craters look like dark circles when you look up at the Moon. Some craters are bigger than your town, and some are smaller than your fingertip. Meteorites have made craters on Earth, too.

▼ **Moon crater**

Craters on Earth

◉ Where craters are on Earth

Rocks The surface of the Moon is covered with **fine gray dust** and sand. There are **pebbles** and **enormous** boulders, too. In fact, the Moon is made up of different kinds of dry rock.

Lava Other dark areas of the Moon were formed long ago by hot, melted rock called lava. This soft, liquid rock covered large areas of the Moon. A long time ago, people on Earth thought these dark areas were seas full of water. Now we know that is not true.

▼ **Lava sometimes flows on Earth today.**

---

fine gray dust very small pieces of dirt
pebbles small rocks
enormous very big

Before You Move On

1. **Details** Name three features on the surface of the Moon.

2. **Comparison** How are the Moon and Earth the same? How are they different?

What Is It Like on the Moon?

Temperature There is air all around Earth, but there is no air around the Moon. Because there is no air on the Moon, the sky always looks black, and there is no sound. Without air, temperatures get very hot during the day (230°F or hotter!) and very cold at night (−315°F or colder).

▼ **The Moon's sky is always black.**

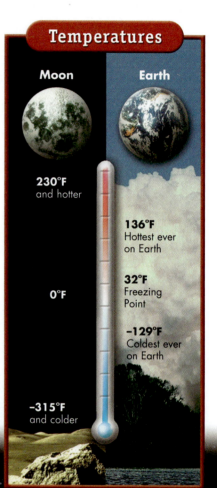

Temperatures

Moon

Earth

230°F
and hotter

136°F
Hottest ever
on Earth

32°F
Freezing
Point

0°F

−129°F
Coldest ever
on Earth

−315°F
and colder

Life Nothing can live on the Moon because there is no air or liquid water. People, plants, and animals all need air and water to live. When **astronauts** go to the Moon in a **spacecraft**, they bring their own air and water. They wear special suits that give them air to breathe. Their suits also keep them cool in the day and warm at night.

Astronaut in
a space suit ▶

Earth's sky looks blue. ▼

Before You Move On

1. **Graphic Aids** How much hotter is the Moon than Earth?

2. **Conclusion** List three things you would need to survive on the Moon.

What Have People Left on the Moon?

Footprints Neil Armstrong and Edwin Aldrin were the first people to walk on the Moon. Because there is no air or wind on the Moon, the footprints they made in 1969 are probably still on the Moon's surface.

▲ Footprint made by an astronaut on the dusty surface of the Moon

Symbols Astronauts have left more than footprints on the Moon. They left behind things that tell about life on Earth. They left a U.S. flag, a falcon feather, a four-leaf clover, and a sign. The sign says:

Here men from the planet Earth
First set foot upon the Moon
July 1969, A.D.
We came in peace for all **mankind**.

Would you like to visit the Moon?
What would you take with you?

Symbols Pictures or objects that represent ideas or things
mankind people

◄ **Astronaut Dave Scott walked on the Moon in 1971. He is one of only twelve astronauts to ever walk on the Moon.**

Before You Move On

1. **Cause/Effect** Why are footprints probably still on the Moon today?

2. **Inference** Why did astronauts leave symbols of Earth on the Moon?

MOON

When I was little
I thought the moon was a white jade plate.
Or maybe a mirror in Heaven
Flying through the blue clouds.

—*Li Bai*

QUIET NIGHT

A moonbeam by my bed
Or frost on the ground?
I look up at the full moon,
I look down and think of home.

—Li Bai

Meet the Poet

Li Bai lived long ago in China. He grew up in one part of China and then left home to explore the rest of the country. He is known as China's best poet, and people still read his poetry today.

Before You Move On

Comparison How are these poems alike? How are they different?

Think and Respond

Strategy: Make Comparisons

Make a comparison chart. Show how the
Moon and Earth are alike and different.

	Moon	Earth
sunlight	✔	✔
mountains		
hills		
valleys		
craters		
rocks		
lava		
air		
water		
plants		
footprints		

Summarize

Use your chart to summarize the article. Tell only
the main ideas and keep your summary short.
Compare your summary to a partner's summary.
Are they alike? Talk about it.

Talk It Over

1 **Personal Response** Imagine you just landed on the Moon. What will you see first?

2 **Cause/Effect** Can people live on the Moon? Why or why not?

3 **Inference** Why do astronauts need space suits on the Moon?

4 **Opinion** Do you think it is important to learn about the Moon? Why or why not?

Compare Topics

Compare what you learned in "The Moon" with what you learned in "The Fox in the Moon."

In "The Moon," I learned facts about the Moon. In "The Fox in the Moon," I learned what people see in the Moon.

171

Content Connections

Talk About History

small group

When Neil Armstrong stepped on the Moon, he said, "That's one small step for a man, one giant leap for mankind." What did he mean? Talk about your ideas with a group.

▲ Neil Armstrong on the Moon in 1969

MATH

Multiply Weights

partners

The force of gravity makes things weigh six times more on Earth than they do on the Moon. Copy and complete this chart on a separate sheet of paper. Use the chart to tell a partner or your family about gravity.

	Moon Weight	Earth Weight
Backpack	2 pounds	
Dog	10 pounds	
Adult	30 pounds	

Make a Display

large group

The astronauts took symbols of Earth to leave on the Moon. If you could visit another planet, what would you take as symbols of Earth? Make a display. Explain each item to your class.

U.S. flag   falcon feather   four-leaf clover

WRITING

Write a Fact Book

Internet

partners

Find more facts about the Moon. Then make a question-and-answer book. Here are some good questions:

• How many miles is the Moon from Earth?

• How big is the Moon?

Share your book with the class.

What is on the surface of the Moon?

There are rocks, boulders, sand, and dust on the Moon.

Plural Nouns

Listen and sing.

Song

WHAT DO THEY SEE?

Astronauts fly to the Moon.

Men and women fly to the Moon.

Astronauts fly to the Moon.

And what do you think they see?

They see mountains down below.

They see valleys down below.

They see craters down below.

And that is what they see.

—*Jane Zion Brauer*

Tune: "Blue-Tail Fly" (Jimmie, Crack Corn)

How Language Works

A **singular noun** shows "one."
A **plural noun** shows "more than one."

How to Make a Noun Plural	Examples:	
1. To make most nouns plural, add **-s**.	dream	dream**s**
2. If the noun ends in **x**, **ch**, **sh**, **s**, or **z**, add **-es**.	fox	fox**es**
3. For nouns that end in a **vowel** plus **y**, just add **-s**.	day	day**s**
4. For most nouns that end in **y**, change the **y** to **i** and add **-es**.	baby	bab**ies**
5. Some nouns do not follow a pattern. They are **irregular**.	foot / child	**feet** / **children**

Practice with a Partner

Make each red noun plural. Then say the sentence.

city   1. Someday there will be _____ on the Moon.

child   2. Adults and _____ could move to the Moon.

box   3. There would be many _____ to bring from Earth.

bush   4. We would have to bring our own trees and _____ .

astronaut   5. We could all be _____ !

Put It in Writing

Pretend that you are an astronaut. You travel to a planet with five moons. Write about your trip.

There are mountains on all of the moons.

Unit 3 Wrap-Up

Show What You Know

Talk About the Moon

In this unit, you read a folk tale and a science article about the Moon. Look back at this unit. Find your favorite picture of the Moon. Tell your group why you like it. Use the picture to tell what you learned about the Moon.

Make a Mind Map

Work with a partner. Make a mind map to show what you learned about the Moon.

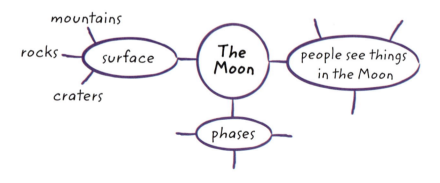

Think and Write

What questions do you still have about the Moon? Make a list. Add the list to your portfolio. Also include work that shows what you learned about the Moon.

Read and Learn More

Leveled Books

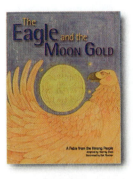

The Eagle and the Moon Gold
by Yeemay Chan

Man on the Moon
by Anastasia Suen

Theme Library

**Moon Rope/
Un lazo a la luna**
by Lois Ehlert

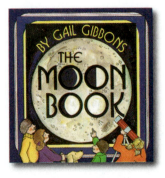

The Moon Book
by Gail Gibbons

Internet

Go to: www.hbavenues.com

Gravity Calculator

Moon Phase Calculator

Crater Map of Earth

The Cycle of Seasons

Draw the Seasons

1. Listen to some music about a season.
2. What season does the music sound like?
3. Draw a picture of that season.
4. Compare drawings with a partner.

The Seasons

The Earth moves around the Sun. Because the Earth tilts, or leans, different parts of the Earth get more sunlight. This is why seasons change.

Northern Hemisphere

Equator

Southern Hemisphere

The Earth is tipped to one side on an imaginary line called the axis.

Sun

▲ When it is summer in the Northern hemisphere, it is winter in the Southern hemisphere.

What Causes Weather?

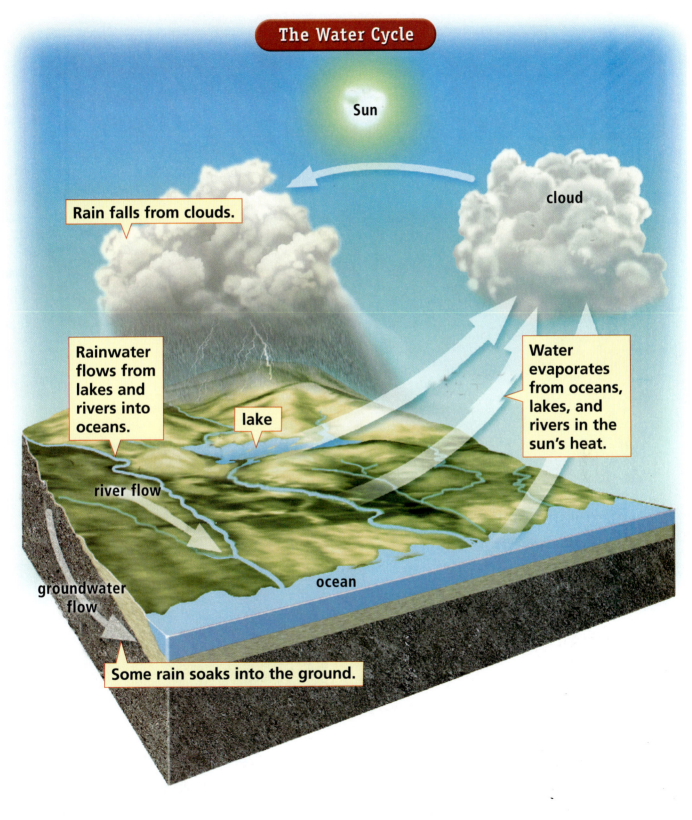

The Water Cycle

Sun

cloud

Rain falls from clouds.

Rainwater flows from lakes and rivers into oceans.

lake

Water evaporates from oceans, lakes, and rivers in the sun's heat.

river flow

groundwater flow

ocean

Some rain soaks into the ground.

A Winter Visit

I went to visit Jasmine in Chicago.
It was snowy **weather**.
I **suffered** from the cold.

We walked around the city.
The sun **refused** to shine.
The snow would not **melt**.

The icy sidewalk was **dangerous**. A **stranger** fell down. Jasmine's mom did not know the man, but she helped him anyway.

Key Words

weather

suffer

refuse

melt

dangerous

stranger

greedy

That night, Jasmine and I had hot chocolate. I tried not to be **greedy**. I only had three cups!

Gluskabe and Old Man Winter

by **Joseph Bruchac**

illustrated by **Pablo Torrecilla**

Read a Play

Genre

A **play** is a story that is acted and read aloud. The written form of a play is a **script**. The script tells about each new setting and what the characters do and say. A play is divided into **scenes**, not chapters.

Characters

Gluskabe

Old Man Winter

Summer Land People

Setting

This story takes place in a forest long ago. It has been winter there for a long time.

▲ forest in winter

Selection Reading

1 It has been winter too long. What does Gluskabe plan to do?

Scene 1:
Gluskabe and Grandmother Woodchuck's Wigwam

Gluskabe and Grandmother Woodchuck sit inside with their blankets over their shoulders.

Narrator: Long ago Gluskabe (gloo-SKAH-bey) lived with his grandmother, Woodchuck, who was old and very **wise**. Gluskabe's job was to help the people.

Gluskabe: It is very cold this winter, Grandmother.

Grandmother Woodchuck: Ni ya yo (nee yah yo), Grandson. You are right!

Gluskabe: The snow is very deep, Grandmother.

Grandmother Woodchuck: *Ni ya yo,* Grandson.

Gluskabe: It has been winter for a very long time, Grandmother.

---

wise smart
Ni ya yo You are right (in the Abenaki language)

186

Grandmother Woodchuck: *Ni ya yo*, Grandson. But look, here comes one of those **human beings** who are our friends.

Human Being: *Kwai, kwai, nidobak* (kwy kwy nee-DOH-bahk). Hello, my friends.

Gluskabe and Grandmother Woodchuck: *Kwai, kwai, nidoba* (kwy kwy nee-DOH-bah).

Human Being: Gluskabe, I have been sent by the other human beings to ask you for help. This winter has been too long. If it does not end soon, we will all die.

Gluskabe: I will do what I can. I will go to the **wigwam** of Old Man Winter. He has stayed here too long. I will ask him to go back to his home in the Winter Land to the north.

Grandmother Woodchuck: Be careful, Gluskabe.

Gluskabe: Don't worry, Grandmother. Winter cannot beat me.

human beings people

Kwai, kwai, nidobak Hello, my friends
(in the Abenaki language)

Kwai, kwai, nidoba Hello, our friend
(in the Abenaki language)

wigwam home

Before You Move On

1. **Details** Who comes to talk to Gluskabe and Grandmother Woodchuck?

2. **Problem/Solution** What is the problem in this story? Why is it a problem?

2

Find out if Old Man Winter will listen to Gluskabe.

Scene 2:
The Wigwam of Old Man Winter

Old Man Winter sits in his wigwam, "warming" his hands over his fire made of ice. The four balls of summer are on one side of the stage. Gluskabe enters stage carrying his bag and stands to the side of the wigwam door. He taps on the wigwam.

Old Man Winter: Who is there!

Gluskabe: It is Gluskabe.

Old Man Winter: Ah, come inside and sit by my fire.
(*Gluskabe enters the wigwam.*)

Gluskabe: The people are **suffering**. You must go back to your home in the Winter Land.

Old Man Winter: Oh, I must, eh? But tell me, do you like my fire?

Gluskabe: I do not like your fire. Your fire is not warm. It is cold.

Old Man Winter: Yes, my fire is made of ice. And so are you! (*Old Man Winter throws his white sheet over Gluskabe. Gluskabe falls down. Old Man Winter stands up.*)

Old Man Winter: No one can **defeat me**! (*Old Man Winter pulls Gluskabe out of the **lodge**. Then he goes back inside and closes the door flap. The Sun comes out and shines on Gluskabe. Gluskabe sits up and looks at the Sun.*)

Gluskabe: Ah, that was a good nap! But I am not going into Old Man Winter's lodge again until I talk with my grandmother. (*Gluskabe begins walking across the stage toward the four balls. Grandmother Woodchuck enters.*)

---

defeat me make me go away
lodge house

Grandmother Woodchuck: It is still winter, Gluskabe! Did Old Man Winter **refuse** to speak to you?

Gluskabe: We spoke, but he did not listen. I will speak to him again; and I will make him listen. But tell me, Grandmother, where does the warm **weather** come from?

Grandmother Woodchuck: It is kept in the Summer Land.

Gluskabe: I will go there and bring summer back here.

Grandmother Woodchuck: Grandson, the Summer Land people are **strange people**. Each of them has one eye. They are also **greedy**. They do not want to share the warm weather. It will be **dangerous**.

Gluskabe: Why will it be dangerous?

Grandmother Woodchuck: The Summer Land people keep the summer in a big pot. They dance around it. Four giant crows guard the pot full of summer. Whenever a **stranger** tries to **steal** summer, those crows fly down and pull off his head!

Gluskabe: Grandmother, I will go to the Summer Land. I will cover up one eye and look like the people there. And I will take these four balls of **sinew** with me. (*Gluskabe picks up the four balls, places them in his bag, and puts the bag over his shoulder.*)

---

strange people different from us
steal take
sinew rope or cord made from the body of an animal

Before You Move On

1. **Details** What does Old Man Winter do when Gluskabe asks him to leave?

2. **Summary** How does Gluskabe plan to get the warm weather?

Gluskabe goes to the Summer Land. What will happen there?

Scene 3:
The Summer Land Village

The Summer Land People are dancing around the pot full of summer. They are singing a snake dance song, following their leader, who shakes a rattle in one hand. Four Crows stand guard around the pot as the people dance.

Summer Land People:

> **Wee gai wah neh** (wee guy wah ney),
> Wee gai wah neh,
> Wee gai wah neh, wee gai wah neh,
> Wee gai wah neh, wee gai wah neh,
> Wee gai wah neh.

(Gluskabe enters, wearing an eye patch and carrying his bag with the balls in it.)

Wee gai wah neh This is fun (in the Abenaki language)

Gluskabe: *Kwai, kwai, nidobak!* Hello, my friends.

(Everyone stops dancing. They gather around Gluskabe.)

Leader of the Summer Land People: Who are you?

Gluskabe: I am not a stranger. I am one of you. See, I have one eye.

Second Summer Land Person: I do not remember you.

Gluskabe: I have been gone a long time.

Third Summer Land Person: He does have only one eye.

Fourth Summer Land Person: Let's welcome him back. Come join in our snake dance.

*The singing and dancing begin again: "Wee gai wah neh," **etc.** Gluskabe is at the end of the line as the dancers circle the pot full of summer. When Gluskabe is close enough, he reaches in, grabs one of the summersticks, and breaks away, running back and forth.*

Leader of the Summer Land People: He has taken one of our summersticks!

Second Summer Land Person: Someone stop him!

Third Summer Land Person: Crows, catch him!

Fourth Summer Land Person: Pull off his head!

---

etc. and so on

*The Crows **swoop** after Gluskabe. He reaches into his*
***pouch** and pulls out one of the balls. As each Crow*
*comes up to him, he **ducks** his head down and holds up*
the ball. The Crow grabs the ball. Gluskabe keeps
running, and pulls out another ball, repeating his actions
until each of the Crows has grabbed a ball.

First Crow: *Gah-gah!* I have his head.

Second Crow: *Gah-gah!* No, I have his head.

Third Crow: *Gah-gah!* Look, I have his head!

Fourth Crow: *Gah-gah!* No, look—I have it, too!

Leader of the Summer Land People: How many
   heads did that stranger have?

Second Summer Land Person: He has tricked us.
   He got away.

Before You Move On

1. **Details** How does Gluskabe use the sinew balls?

2. **Prediction** Do you think Gluskabe will solve the human beings' problem? Why or why not?

4

Read to find out if Gluskabe defeats Old Man Winter.

Scene 4:
The Wigwam of Old Man Winter

Gluskabe walks up to Old Man Winter's wigwam. He holds the summerstick in his hand and taps on the door.

Old Man Winter: Who is there!

Gluskabe: It is Gluskabe.

Old Man Winter: Ah, come inside and sit by my fire.

(Gluskabe enters, sits down, and places the summerstick in front of Old Man Winter.)

Gluskabe: You must go back to your home in the Winter Land.

Old Man Winter: Oh, I must, eh? But tell me, do you like my fire?

Gluskabe: Your fire is no longer cold. It is getting warmer. Your wigwam is **melting** away. You are getting weaker.

Old Man Winter: No one can defeat me!

Gluskabe: Old Man, you are defeated. Warm weather has returned. Go back to your home in the north.

(*The blanket walls of Old Man Winter's wigwam* **collapse**. *Old Man Winter stands up and walks away as* **swiftly** *as he can,* **crouching down** *as if getting smaller. People carrying the cutouts of the Sun, Flowers, and Plants come out and surround Gluskabe as he sits there, smiling.*)

Narrator: So Gluskabe defeated Old Man Winter. Because he brought only one small piece of summer, winter still returns each year. But, thanks to Gluskabe, spring always comes back again.

---

collapse fall
swiftly quickly
crouching down bending over

Before You Move On

1. **Problem/Solution** How do you know Old Man Winter is defeated?

2. **Summary** Tell what happens in Scene 4.

Joseph Bruchac

AWARD WINNER

Joseph Bruchac grew up in his grandparents' home in New York. His grandfather was from the Native American tribe of Abenaki. He taught young Joseph many lessons about the natural world. Mr. Bruchac remembers, "I learned how to tell what time of year it was by the things that were happening around us." Winter was the time for storytelling.

Today, Mr. Bruchac is a famous storyteller, writer, and poet. He feels it is important to share the stories he has learned from other Native Americans.

Think and Respond

Strategy: Problem and Solution

Some stories tell how a character solves a problem. In these stories, look for the:

- ✔ problem
- ✔ events
- ✔ solution.

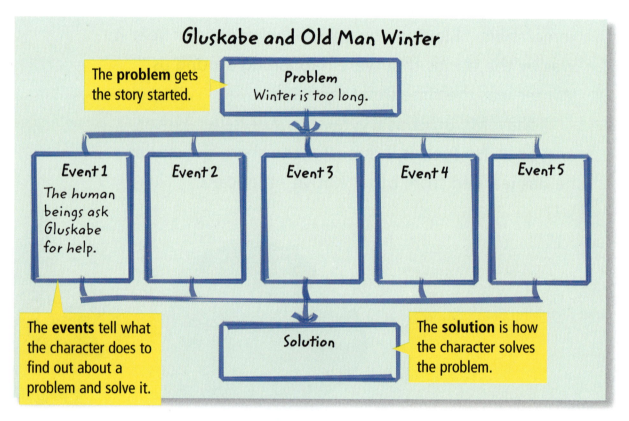

Gluskabe and Old Man Winter

The **problem** gets the story started.

Problem
Winter is too long.

Event 1
The human beings ask Gluskabe for help.

Event 2

Event 3

Event 4

Event 5

The **events** tell what the character does to find out about a problem and solve it.

Solution

The **solution** is how the character solves the problem.

Make a problem and solution chart for "Gluskabe and Old Man Winter."

Retell the Story

Retell the story to a partner. Does your retelling match your partner's? What was different? Talk about it.

Talk It Over

1 **Personal Response** What would you tell a friend about this story? Why?

2 **Judgment** Do you think Gluskabe's solution was the best way to solve the problem? Why or why not?

3 **Speculate** How might this story be different if the Summer Land People told it? If Old Man Winter told it?

4 **Genre** The story of "Gluskabe and Old Man Winter" has been told for many, many years. It is a legend. Tell your partner a legend that you know.

Compare Genres

Compare this play to "The Fox in the Moon." How are plays and stories different?

Content Connections

Give Messages

Make up a message to give Gluskabe. Tell it to a partner. Your partner gives the message to Gluskabe. Then Gluskabe says the message aloud.

Did your message change? Explain.

Gluskabe, the Human Beings need help.

small group

SOCIAL STUDIES

partners

Compare Legends

Internet

Read other Native American legends. Make a chart. Decide which legend you like best and which you like least. Share your ideas with the class.

Legend	Hero	Problem	Solution
Gluskabe and Old Man Winter	Gluskabe	Winter is too long.	

Create the Water Cycle

large group

You will need a saucepan with a lid, a burner, an oven mitt, and water.

1. Fill the saucepan with water.
2. Put it on the burner.
3. Bring the water to a boil.
4. Put on the oven mitt and hold the lid over the saucepan.
   What happens? Talk about it.

Write a Description

small group

Choose one of the characters from the play. Pretend you are that person and write a description of another character. Can your group guess who you are?

> Gluskabe is funny-looking. He has two eyes instead of one. He is also a mean man. He takes things from others.

Make Inferences

When you read and **make inferences**, you make good guesses. To make inferences:

✔ Read carefully.
✔ Think about what the writer says.
✔ Use what you know and other clues to guess what the writer means.

Try the strategy.

from *Gluskabe and Old Man Winter*

Gluskabe: You must go back to your home in the Winter Land.

Old Man Winter: Oh, I must, eh? But tell me, do you like my fire?

Gluskabe: Your fire is no longer cold. It is getting warmer. Your wigwam is melting away. You are getting weaker.

Old Man Winter is getting weak. That must mean that winter will end soon.

Practice

Take this test and <mark>make inferences</mark> about "Gluskabe and Old Man Winter."

Read each item. Choose the best answer.

1 **Why do you think the human beings wanted winter to end?**

   ⬭ They lived in small wigwams.

   ⬭ They were Summer Land People.

   ⬭ They were afraid of the four crows.

   ⬭ They needed to grow more food to eat.

2 **Why did Grandmother Woodchuck tell Gluskabe to be careful?**

   ⬭ The Sun was very powerful.

   ⬭ The human beings were suffering.

   ⬭ She did not trust Old Man Winter.

   ⬭ Gluskabe wanted to go to the Winter Land.

✔ Test Strategy

Read parts of the play again. Then choose your answer.

3 **You can tell from the play that Gluskabe was—**

   ⬭ tall

   ⬭ quiet

   ⬭ clever

   ⬭ greedy

Song

The Four Seasons

Summer

Can you feel the wind
Blow through the leaves?
Can you feel the **sunlight**
And the summer **breeze**?

Autumn

In red and golden forests,
The dying leaves **fall**.
Every season **changes**.
Hear the wild bird call.

Tune: "Los pollitos"
(The Baby Chicks)

212

Winter

Touch the snowy **branches**.
Ice is underneath.
Clouds are gray and full.
Everything's asleep.

Spring

After the long winter,
Birds begin to sing.
Then **frost** **disappears**
And new life begins.

—Maria Del Rey

Key Words

sunlight

breeze

fall

change

branch

cloud

frost

disappear

Read an Art Essay

An **art essay** is nonfiction. It uses art to tell about a topic.

✔ Study the **paintings,** or **illustrations,** to see what the essay is about.

✔ Use the **captions** to find out more about the illustration.

painting

caption

What does this painting show us about autumn colors?

Selection Reading

Sky Tree

by Thomas Locker

Set Your Purpose

Read for details. How does a tree change during each season?

Once a tree stood alone on a hill by the river. Through the long days, its leaves **fluttered** in the soft summer **breeze**.

When you look at this painting of the tree on a hill, can you remember how you felt on a **perfect** summer day?

---

fluttered moved
perfect nice, wonderful

216

But then the days grew shorter and the nights longer. The winds became cold, and the tree began to **change**.

This is the same tree in the same place.
What makes this painting different?

Autumn came. The leaves of the tree turned gold, orange, and red. Squirrels hurried to store nuts and acorns.

What does this painting show us about autumn colors?

The sun rose later each day. One morning, light **glistened** on a thin silver <mark>**frost**</mark>. By the end of the day, many leaves began to <mark>**fall**</mark>, first one and then another.

Why does this painting make you feel sad?
Is the tree dying?

---

glistened shone

On a grey day, an old snapping turtle buried herself in the river mud, where she would sleep until spring. The tree's **bare branches** reached toward the sky. The **clouds opened**, and for a moment, the sky **filled the branches**.

Why is this painting so strange and **startling**?

bare branches empty branches
clouds opened clouds separated
filled the branches looked like the leaves of the tree
startling surprising

snapping turtle ▶

On a **misty** morning, a **flock** of birds landed where the tree's leaves had been. The birds chirped, squabbled, and sang, but suddenly **their wings beat the air**, and they flew away.

How does this painting **capture the feeling** of a misty day?

---

misty wet
flock group
their wings beat the air they made a noise as they moved their wings
capture the feeling make you think

Clouds **gathered and filled** the tree's empty branches and then **drifted** away.

How does this painting show how water in the air changes the way we see things?

gathered and filled came together and seemed to cover

drifted went

Ice formed on the river's edge. With its roots deep in the earth, the tree stood ready for winter.

Does this painting make you feel as if something is about to happen?

Snows fell. **Snug** in their nest, a family of squirrels **huddled close** through the cold winter days.

How does this painting capture the **stillness** of a snowy day?

▼ **squirrels**

Snug Warm
huddled close stayed very close to each other
stillness silence, quiet

At night, millions of stars **twinkled** among the branches of the tree. Beneath the river ice, the old snapping turtle slept. The world was waiting for spring.

Does this painting make you feel small?

---

twinkled shone, sparkled

Late one afternoon, **a golden light streamed** through the clouds and warmed the tree. The ice on the river began to melt, and the snow ==disappeared== into the ground.

How does this painting show that winter is ending?

∞

<hr>

a golden light streamed the sun shone

The smell of wet earth filled the air. Squirrels raced through the fresh grass and up the tree. **Sap** rose to the tree's tight **buds**.

Does this painting make you feel **hopeful**?

Sap Sticky juice inside the tree
buds tiny new leaves
hopeful that something good might happen

The old **snapper** crawled out of the mud to lay her eggs on the warm hillside. The tree's leaves **uncurled** in the spring <mark>sunlight</mark>, and the birds returned to build nests for their young.

Now the tree is full and round again.
What does this painting make you feel about summer?

snapper turtle
uncurled opened

birds and their
babies in a nest ▶

The tree stood on the hill by the river. Once again, its leaves fluttered in the soft summer breeze.

Why do you think this essay is called "Sky Tree"?

Meet the Author and Illustrator

Thomas Locker

AWARD WINNER

Thomas Locker loves to paint trees. When he was seven years old, he painted a picture of a tree and won first prize at an art fair.

Mr. Locker started writing picture books because he wanted to share his love of nature with children. He decided to paint pictures of a tree outside his studio window. These paintings became the book *Sky Tree.*

Think and Respond

Strategy: Classify Details

Make a cycle diagram. Give details about the plants, animals, and weather for each season.

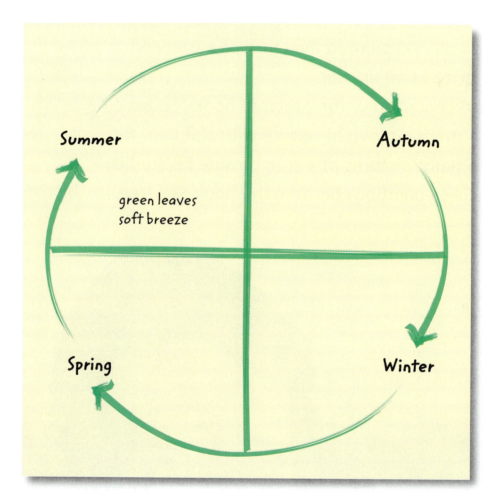

Summarize

Say a sentence to summarize each season. Use the most important details about the season in your sentence.

Talk It Over

1 **Personal Response** What is your favorite season? Why?

2 **Author's Purpose** Why did the author paint pictures of the same tree over and over again?

3 **Opinion** Do you think reading an art essay is a good way to learn about seasons? Why or why not?

4 **Viewing** What are some ways the artist shows how the seasons change?

Compare Visuals

Compare the tree paintings in "Sky Tree" to photographs of trees.

A painting can show details that are not real, but a photo shows what is really there.

233

Content Connections

Picture the Season

Internet

on your own

Look on the Internet for art of nature. Print some. Use paint, crayons, clay, or other materials to show the scene in a different season. Describe your work to the class.

Charles De Wolf Brownell, "Cuban Landscape," oil on canvas, 1866

MATH

Chart the Temperature

partners

1. Choose a city from the weather page in the newspaper.

2. Record the temperature for a week.

3. Make a line graph.

4. What can you say about the city's weather?

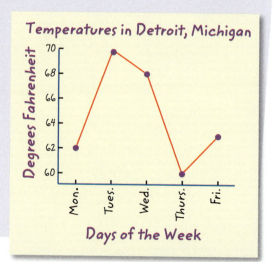

Temperatures in Detroit, Michigan

Degrees Fahrenheit

70
68
66
64
62
60

Mon. Tues. Wed. Thurs. Fri.

Days of the Week

Play a Seasons Game

large group

Make two piles of cards. Names of countries go in one pile, and the names of months go in the other.

- Choose a card from each pile.
- Use the map to tell where the country is.
- What clothes would you take to that country during that season? Why?

> I would take my swim suit to Australia in December. It is summer.

WRITING

Write to Entertain

on your own

Think about what the seasons are like. Write about one season. Choose the best form:

- a poem
- a story.

Choose words that help your readers "see" what things look like.

> I love to be outside on hot summer days. I pick red strawberries from the round pots on our tiny balcony. Then I sit in the cool shade next to our apartment steps and eat the juicy berries.

Pronouns

Listen and sing.

Song

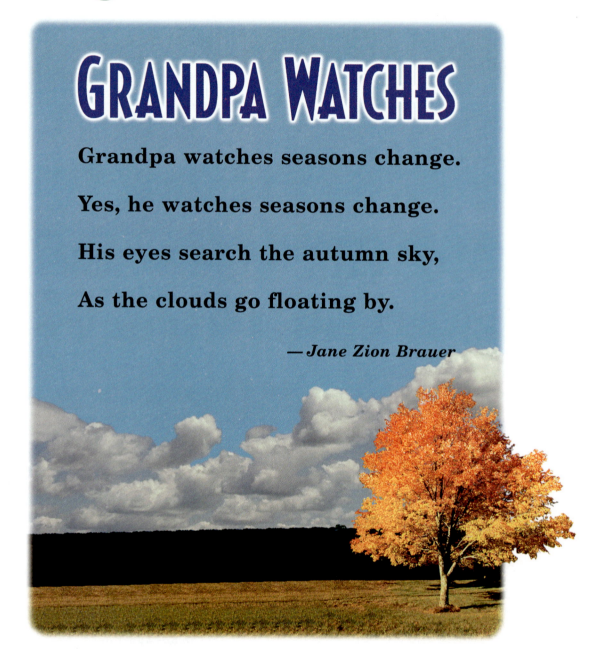

GRANDPA WATCHES

Grandpa watches seasons change.

Yes, he watches seasons change.

His eyes search the autumn sky,

As the clouds go floating by.

—*Jane Zion Brauer*

Tune: "Come, Dreams"

236

How Language Works

A **pronoun** can take the place of a noun.

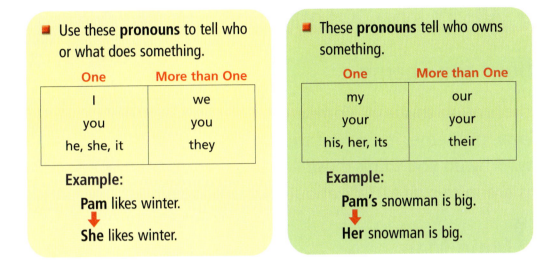

- Use these **pronouns** to tell who or what does something.

One	More than One
I	we
you	you
he, she, it	they

Example:

Pam likes winter.

She likes winter.

- These **pronouns** tell who owns something.

One	More than One
my	our
your	your
his, her, its	their

Example:

Pam's snowman is big.

Her snowman is big.

Practice with a Partner

Choose the correct red pronoun. Then say the sentence.

she / her   1. Pam and _____ pals wait under a tree.

She / Her   2. _____ smiles at them.

They / Their   3. _____ look up at the tree.

it / its   4. Snow covers _____ branches.

they / their   5. Some snow falls on _____ heads!

Put It in Writing

Write about your favorite season. Tell what you and your family like to do at that time.

I swim in the summer.

Show What You Know

Talk About the Theme

Look back through this unit. Compare the big idea, or theme, in each of the selections. Why do you think these selections are in this unit? Talk about it with a partner.

Make a Mind Map

Work with a partner. Make a mind map to show what you learned about seasons.

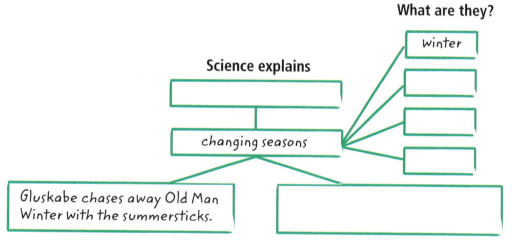

What are they?

winter

Science explains

changing seasons

Gluskabe chases away Old Man Winter with the summersticks.

People show

Think and Write

What questions can you answer about seasons? Write the question and then the answer. Add this writing to your portfolio. Include work from this unit that shows what you learned about seasons.

Read and Learn More

Leveled Books

In the Yard
by Dana Meachen Rau

The Wind Eagle
by Joyce McGreevy

Theme Library

**A Tree for
All Seasons**
by Robin Bernard

**The Winter King
and the
Summer Queen**
by Mary Lister

Internet

Go to: www.hbavenues.com

Reason for the Seasons

Water Cycle

Art Galleries

CACTUS AND CANYONS

Compare Sand and Soil

1. Fill one pot with dirt. Fill another pot with sand. Put each pot in a bowl.
2. Pour one cup of water into each pot.
3. Measure the water that goes into each bowl.
4. Is sand or soil better for a plant?

A Desert Ecosystem

cactus

arch

mountains

scorpion

mountain lion

Landforms

mountain

canyon

valley

plateau

lake

plain

hill

river

coast

peninsula

island

ocean

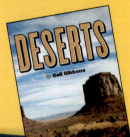
Song

Gila Monster

I am a Gila monster.
I love my **sandy** **dunes**.
I love my **rocky** home.

I am a **reptile** who moves slowly.
I go creeping across
This hot **desert floor**.

I **adapt** well without water.
I find **protection** from the sun
And hunt my **prey** all night.
I am a Gila monster.

—*Maria Del Rey*

Key Words

sandy

dune

rocky

reptile

desert floor

adapt

protection

prey

Read a Science Article

A **science article** is nonfiction. It gives facts about a topic.

✔ Look for **diagrams** with numbered steps. They show how things work.

numbered step

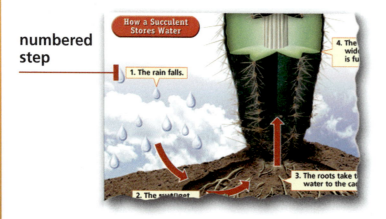

How a Succulent Stores Water

1. The rain falls.

2. The water get

3. The roots take the water to the ca

4. The wid is fu

✔ Read the **table**, **graphs**, and **maps** to find facts.

Selection Reading

DESERTS

by **Gail Gibbons**

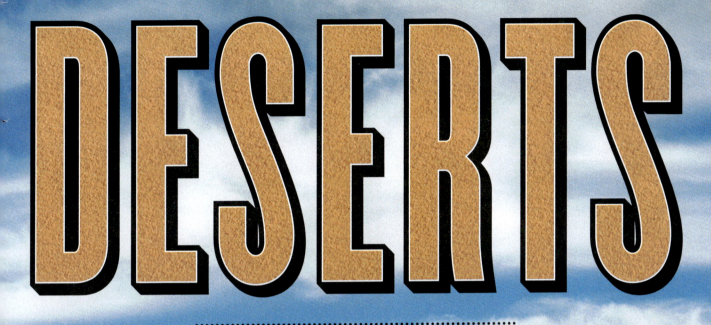

Set Your Purpose

Find out what deserts are like. What lives there?

Kinds of Deserts

It is hot, and the sky is clear. It is daytime in the desert. A desert is a place that is very dry. In most deserts it rains less than ten inches a year.

Average Yearly Rainfall	
California desert	2.0 inches
New Mexico desert	8.5 inches
Houston, Texas	46.0 inches
New York City	47.0 inches

▼ **Monument Valley, Arizona**

Deserts can be **sandy** or **rocky**. About one-fifth of all deserts are sandy. Over many years wind and other **elements** wore away and broke down rocks into tiny **grains** of sand. Sandy deserts can look different. Some sandy **desert floors** look like rippled water. Wind blows the sand and **changes the sand's appearance**.

---

elements types of weather

grains bits

changes the sand's appearance makes the sand look different

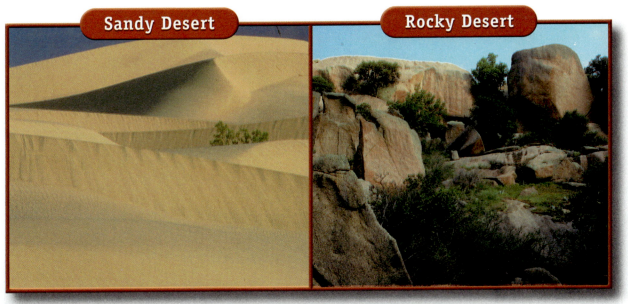

Sandy Desert

Rocky Desert

▲ **Death Valley, California**

▲ **Southern Colorado**

◄ **The wind made little waves in this desert sand.**

Before You Move On

1. **Graphic Aids** What is the yearly rainfall of a New Mexico desert?

2. **Inference** What clothing is good to wear in a desert? Why?

249

Other sandy deserts **look uneven and lumpy**. If something is in the sand's way, sand piles up behind it. On some sandy deserts strong winds blow the sand into smooth hills called <mark>dunes</mark>. Over time dunes can move.

---

look uneven and lumpy are full of bumps

◀ **The wind blows the sand into little piles behind these plants.**

▼**Death Valley, California**

sand dune

Rocky deserts can look different and very **strange**. Often wind-blown sand **wears** rocks into odd shapes. Many deserts have jagged rocks. Sudden rains, along with heat and cold, crack the rocks and pieces break away.

---

strange odd
wears changes

A rocky desert in Northeastern Arizona ▶

jagged rocks

Before You Move On

1. **Comparison** Tell two ways rocky deserts and sandy deserts are different.

2. **Opinion** Which type of desert would you like to visit? Why?

251

Plants and Animals in the Desert

Few plants and animals can live in the desert because it is so dry and hot. The ones that do live there have **adapted** to living without much water. Many plants that live in the desert are called succulents. They take rainwater up through their roots to store in their leaves or stems for use during dry, hot **spells**.

---

spells times

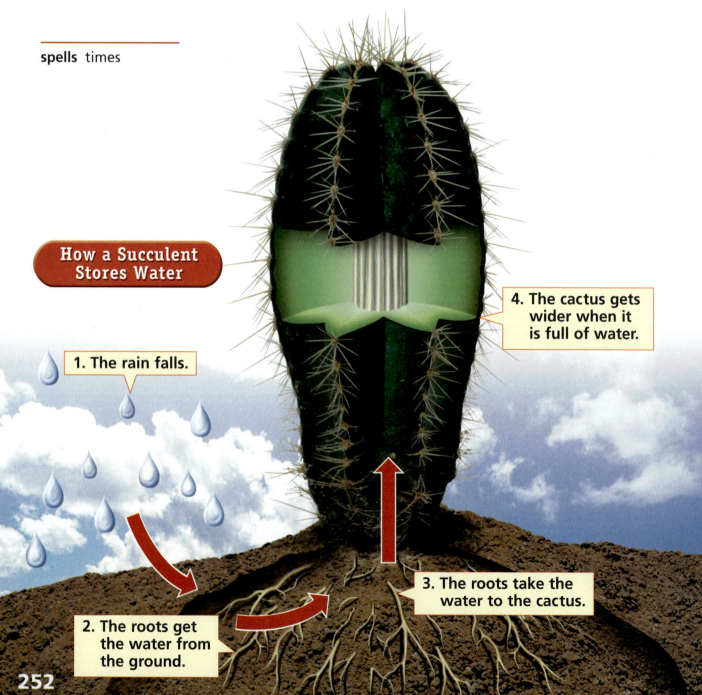

How a Succulent Stores Water

1. The rain falls.

2. The roots get the water from the ground.

3. The roots take the water to the cactus.

4. The cactus gets wider when it is full of water.

▲ **Desert wildflowers in the Sonoran Desert, Arizona**

In some deserts when it finally does rain, parts of the desert can be covered in desert flowers. They have grown from seeds that may have been lying there for many years. These seeds grow into plants when there is just the right amount of rain at the right time of year.

Before You Move On

1. **Graphic Aids** Describe how a succulent stores water.

2. **Details** How do plants adapt to living in the desert?

Lizards and snakes move along the desert floor. Lizards and snakes are **reptiles**. A reptile is a cold-blooded animal that crawls or moves on its belly or on its short legs.

Some desert snakes are dangerous. They hunt mice, lizards, birds, and other small animals. Some bite with a **poisonous** venom and swallow their **prey**.

---

poisonous dangerous. Something poisonous can make you sick.

▼ A snake prepares to bite its prey.

How Reptiles Protect Themselves

▲ The horned lizard is covered with sharp points for **protection** .

▲ The Gila monster uses poison to protect itself.

▲ The Inland Taipan has a poisonous bite.

▲ The fringe-toed lizard can dig itself into the sand for protection within seconds to **escape enemies**.

---

escape enemies get away from animals that might eat it

Before You Move On

1. **Graphic Aids** Name two reptiles. Tell something about each one.

2. **Inference** Why do you think some desert reptiles are brown?

Some desert birds live in cactus plants. Sometimes pairs of Gila woodpeckers **nest** inside a tall saguaro cactus. When they **abandon** the nest, other birds such as the elf owl move in.

Vultures are very big desert birds. They live off dead animals. They are **scavengers** and help keep the desert clean.

---

nest make their homes
abandon leave
scavengers animals that eat only dead things

Gila woodpecker

vulture

saguaro cactus

elf owl

desert floor

The roadrunner is a very fast desert bird. It runs quickly to catch insects, lizards, and snakes. It hardly ever flies. The roadrunner can run as fast as seventeen miles an hour.

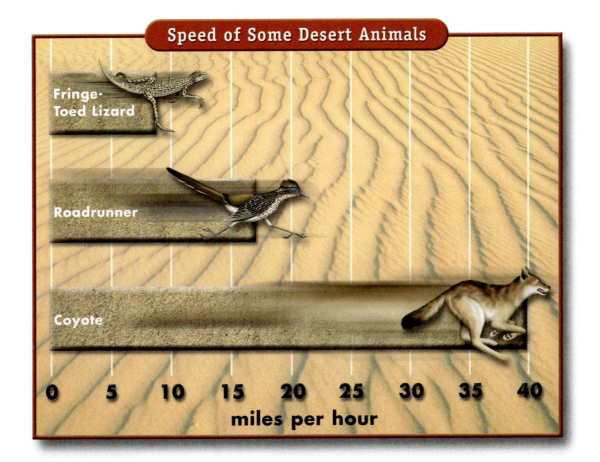

Speed of Some Desert Animals

Fringe-Toed Lizard

Roadrunner

Coyote

0   5   10   15   20   25   30   35   40

miles per hour

Before You Move On

1. **Classify** Sort the animals from pages 254–257 in two groups: birds and reptiles.

2. **Inference** How does a roadrunner protect itself?

257

jackrabbit

Other desert **creatures** move about. A jackrabbit doesn't need to drink much water. It gets most of its water from the plants it eats. A jackrabbit can leap fifteen feet at a time!

Desert creatures have to watch out for coyotes. Coyotes look a lot like a dog with a **bushy** tail. They bark, howl, and whimper to communicate with other coyotes. At night a coyote's **howl** sounds lonely.

---

creatures animals
bushy big, fluffy
howl cry

▲ Coyotes often travel together.

258

Desert skunks eat almost anything. Many deserts are home for badgers, ground squirrels, bobcats, and many other animals. Most of them are small. There isn't enough food and water in the desert for most large wild animals to **survive**.

---

survive live

▲ **A badger looks for food.**

Before You Move On

1. **Inference** How do you think a jackrabbit stays alive in the desert?

2. **Cause/Effect** Why don't most large animals live in the desert?

Where Do You Find Deserts?

Deserts in the World

ASIA

EUROPE

NORTH AMERICA

AFRICA

SOUTH AMERICA

AUSTRALIA

DESERTS

ANTARCTICA

Deserts cover one-fifth of Earth's land surface. Deserts have some of the most interesting **landscapes** in the world. These dry, rocky, and sandy places are home to many plants and animals. Deserts are **alive with mystery and beauty**.

---

landscapes views of land
alive with mystery and beauty very interesting and beautiful

Before You Move On

1. **Graphic Aids** Where in the world do you see the most deserts?

2. **Opinion** Do you agree that deserts are interesting? Why?

Meet The Author

GAIL GIBBONS

AWARD WINNER

Gail Gibbons didn't know much about desert life before she wrote *Deserts*, so she went to the desert to learn more. "When I first got there," she says, "I thought the desert was empty! I was used to seeing the green trees of my home in Vermont."

Day by day, Ms. Gibbons discovered all the beautiful things that give the desert so much color and life. She says, "Now that I'm back in Vermont, I miss the silence and space that make the desert such an amazing place."

Think and Respond

Strategy: Classify

Make a web. Classify information about the desert.

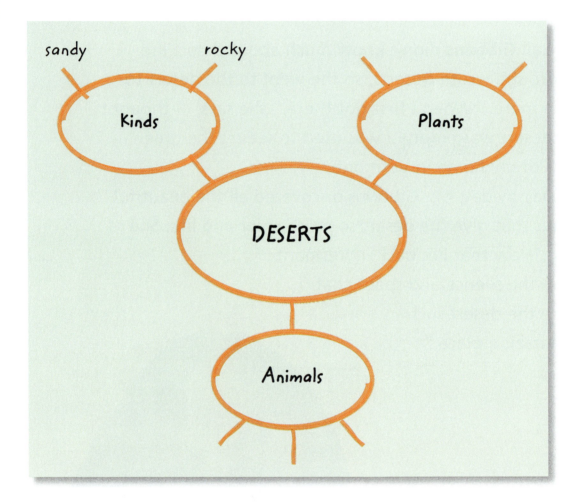

Summarize

Use your web to say three summary sentences: one about the kinds of deserts, one about desert animals, and one about desert plants. Share your sentences with a partner.

Talk It Over

1 **Personal Response** Tell a partner the most interesting thing you learned about the desert.

2 **Inference** Why don't pets like dogs or cats live on their own in the desert?

3 **Comparison** How are the plants and animals in a desert different from those in a city or town?

4 **Author's Point of View** Do you think the author likes the desert? Why or why not?

Compare Topics

Compare what you learned about plants from "How a Plant Grows" and "Deserts."

I learned that plants can live in sand from both science articles.

Content Connections

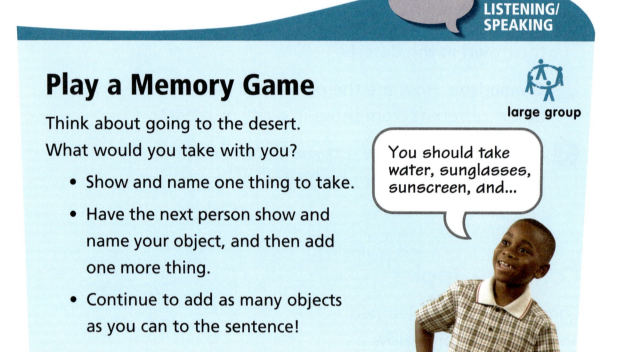

large group

Play a Memory Game

Think about going to the desert. What would you take with you?

- Show and name one thing to take.

- Have the next person show and name your object, and then add one more thing.

- Continue to add as many objects as you can to the sentence!

You should take water, sunglasses, sunscreen, and...

SOCIAL STUDIES

small group

Research Landforms

Compare desert landforms to the landforms of another ecosystem. Make a chart. Show the landforms in the desert. Then research another ecosystem and take notes. Talk about your chart with another group.

Desert and Ocean Landforms		
Desert	Ocean	Both
arches	reefs	canyons
mesas	islands	valleys

Draw a Diagram

Internet

partners

1. Find out more about a desert plant or animal.

2. Draw a diagram of it.

3. Explain your diagram to your group.

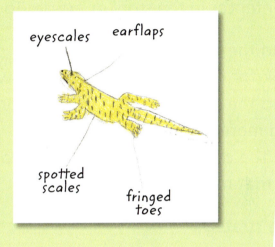

eyescales   earflaps

spotted scales

fringed toes

WRITING

Write Paragraphs

on your own

Write two paragraphs to compare the desert ecosystem with the ecosystem where you live. Tell how the ecosystems are the same and different. Share your paragraphs with a partner.

Desert and forest landforms are very different. There are mesas in the desert but not in the forest.

Use Context Clues

Context clues can help you figure out the meaning of a word you don't know. Context clues are the other words and sentences in the story or article. To **use context clues**:

✔ Read the sentence again.
✔ Look for clues, or hints, about the word's meaning.
✔ Read the sentences that come before and after to find more clues.
✔ Use the clues to guess a meaning for the word.
✔ Try that meaning in the sentence.

Try the strategy.

THE OCOTILLO

The ocotillo is a desert plant that grows in rocky areas. This plant has thin, straight branches covered with spines, or sharp points. Ocotillos may have 75 canes, or branches, when they are fully grown.

Ocotillos bloom annually. Each year, tiny red flowers grow on the branches. The flowers are shaped like long tubes.

I'm not sure what the word *annually* means. The next sentence gives me a good clue. Annually must mean "each year."

Practice

Take this test and <mark>use context clues</mark>.

Read each item. Choose the best answer.

1 **Read the passage.**

> On some sandy deserts strong winds blow the sand into smooth hills called dunes. Over time <u>dunes</u> can move.

Which words best help you understand what <u>dunes</u> means?

- ⬭ on some
- ⬭ smooth hills
- ⬭ over time
- ⬭ can move

✔ **Test Strategy**

Look for key words like *which* and *what*. They will help you find the correct answer.

2 **Read the passage.**

> Many plants that live in the desert are called <u>succulents</u>. They take rainwater up through their roots to store in their leaves or stems for use during hot, dry spells.

What is a <u>succulent</u>?

- ⬭ a kind of desert
- ⬭ a plant without roots
- ⬭ a plant that stores water
- ⬭ a certain kind of rainwater

Almost Lost

Act out the scenes.

Look! I **found** some roadrunner **tracks**! They go into the **gully**.

Let's follow them!

There goes the roadrunner. It's running into the **canyon**.

Wait! I dropped our trail **map**. We'll have to go back and **search** for it so we don't get **lost**.

Key Words

found

tracks

gully

canyon

map

search

lost

Lost

by Paul Brett Johnson
and Celeste Lewis

illustrated by
Paul Brett Johnson

Read a Story

Genre

An <mark>adventure story</mark> is exciting and sometimes scary. In this story, a dog named Flag gets lost in the desert. A girl and her dad look for him.

Characters

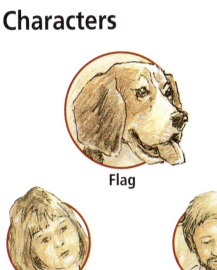

Flag

girl

her dad

Setting

This story happens in a desert in Arizona over many weeks.

Arizona

 Selection Reading

Flag is lost.
What do the
girl and her
dad do?

The day Flag got **lost** in the desert, Dad and I **searched** for him until sundown.

We **found** some dog **tracks** at a **watering hole** and some other tracks, too— big scary ones.

But we didn't find Flag.

watering hole place where animals come to drink

Monday morning I made a **lost-dog poster**. It said, *REWARD: $8.48*. That's how much I had in my **piggy bank**. I hoped it would be enough.

Dad took my poster to work and made copies. After school we drove out into the desert again, passing them out along the way.

lost-dog poster sign to ask people if they have seen my lost dog
piggy bank pig-shaped bank

Finally, three days later, someone called. A lady had found a lost beagle. I couldn't wait till we got to her house. Flag was going to be so happy.

But it wasn't Flag.

I sat beside the **strange dog** and **stroked** his head. I gave him the **biscuit** I had brought.

strange dog dog I didn't know
stroked rubbed
biscuit dog cookie

Before bed I got out my photos of Flag. I couldn't help crying. But I laughed some, too.

The picture of Flag catching lima beans was my favorite. That was Flag's best trick. I hate lima beans, so Flag got mine. Every time I threw one in the air, he would catch it.

Once he caught sixteen in a row!

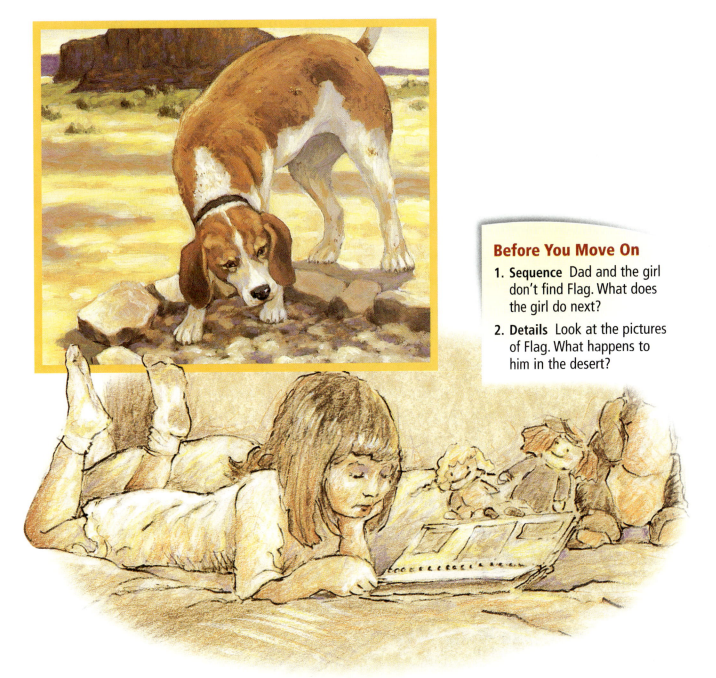

Before You Move On

1. **Sequence** Dad and the girl don't find Flag. What does the girl do next?

2. **Details** Look at the pictures of Flag. What happens to him in the desert?

2

What happens
next? How
does the girl
feel?

The next day Dad came home with a big **map**. It had a million **squiggly** lines that showed every **ridge** and **gully**.

Dad thought Cave Creek **Canyon** would be a good place to look for Flag.

---

squiggly crooked
ridge hill and mountain top

The canyon was **rough going**. We had to crawl on all fours over huge rocks and through **prickly underbrush**.

---

rough going difficult to walk through
prickly underbrush plants with sharp leaves

Suddenly there was **a howl** that sounded just
like Flag. We started yelling his name. *"Flag! Flag!"*

We kept on calling and listening. But all we
heard were our own **voices echoing back at us**.

a howl an animal cry
voices echoing back at us words being repeated

At school I couldn't **concentrate**, even though we were studying **astronomy**, which I really like. There was a big cactus just outside the window. It made me think of the desert and Flag.

Where was he?

I missed him so much.

concentrate focus on my work
astronomy the subject of outer space

Before You Move On

1. **Sequence** Order the events: go in the canyon, call for Flag, look at a map.

2. **Opinion** Do you think the girl really hears Flag howling? Why or why not?

Flag is still lost. Will the girl and her dad give up?

Friday came at last. Dad had promised we could look for Flag again.

But **the whole weekend turned out to be a big fat zero**. All we saw was a **pack of javelinas**. Dad said they could be mean, so we **steered clear**.

I hated the desert!

---

the whole weekend turned out to be a big fat zero we didn't find Flag all weekend

pack of javelinas group of wild pigs

steered clear stayed away from them

Next time out we climbed a fire tower. I knew Flag was somewhere below, looking for me just as hard as I was looking for him. But where?

There was so much ground still to cover.

Please, Flag. Don't give up!

There was so much ground still to cover
We had many more places to look for Flag

Later we met an old **prospector**. He said
he once had a dog that got lost in the desert, but
he never found him. He said it didn't look good
for Flag.

I told him if any dog could make it, Flag could.

We gave him our address and phone number,
just in case.

prospector man who looks for things like
gold or silver

Friday night there was a knock on my door. Dad came into the room and sat beside me on the bed. He took my hand. He said we had to talk.

I knew then we wouldn't be packing up and **heading out** to the desert anymore. Flag had been lost almost a month.

Dad? Please? Flag's still out there. He is waiting for us to come find him. I know he is.

heading out going

283

At breakfast Dad said maybe we should go to the animal shelter and look for another beagle. But I didn't want another beagle. I wanted Flag. Dad was just trying to cheer us both up, I guess.

I marked another X on the calendar. I hoped Flag didn't think I had forgotten him.

Monday when I got home from school, there was a truck in the driveway. I **recognized** the old man we had met in the desert.

I began to run.

Flag was all scratched up, and he was **down to skin and bones**. I hated to think what he must have gone through. He was **bad off**, the prospector said, but he would be fine.

recognized saw
down to skin and bones very, very thin
bad off very sick

When I took Flag in my arms, he **wriggled** a little and tried to lick my face.

I reached in my pocket and showed him what I had been keeping—a dried lima bean.

"For good luck," I whispered. "I never gave up hope."

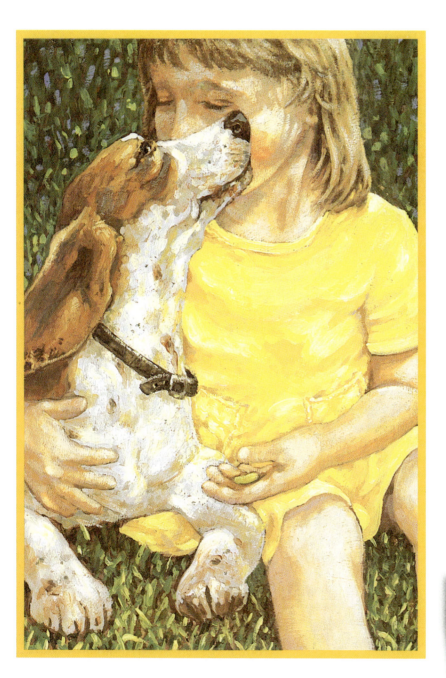

---

wriggled moved

Before You Move On

1. **Character** Why does the girl carry a dried lima bean?

2. **Prediction** Do you think the girl will take Flag to the desert again? Why or why not?

Meet the Author and Illustrator

Paul Brett Johnson

AWARD WINNER

Paul Brett Johnson has written many children's books, but *Lost* is the first one he and Celeste Lewis wrote together. Ms. Lewis really had a dog named Flag who got lost in the desert. When she told Mr. Johnson the story, *Lost* was born.

Mr. Johnson visits schools to teach students how he writes and illustrates books. He even has the students think of story ideas and then helps them to make books.

Think and Respond

Strategy: Sequence of Events

Events in a story happen in a certain order, or sequence. To understand the sequence, look for:

- ✔ the time of day something happens, like *Monday* or *at breakfast*
- ✔ words like *before*, *after*, *next*, *then*, and *finally*.

Make a time line for "Lost." Show the events in order.

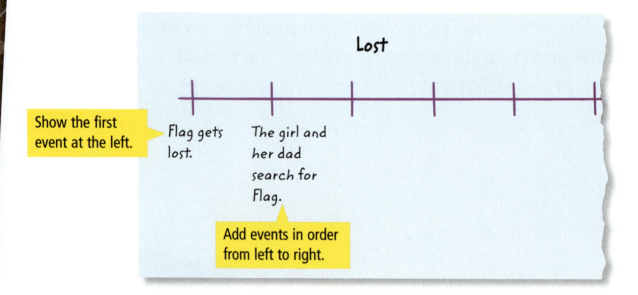

Show the first event at the left.

Flag gets lost.

The girl and her dad search for Flag.

Add events in order from left to right.

Retell the Story

Use your time line to retell the story to a partner. Use sequence words.

Talk It Over

1 **Personal Response** Do you think this story is terrific, just OK, or boring? Why?

2 **Speculate** How would this story be different if it took place in a forest? At the beach?

3 **Author's Purpose** Why did the author include pictures of Flag in the desert?

4 **Character** Tell why you think Flag survived in the desert.

Compare Text and Art

Choose a page in "Lost." Read the words and look at the pictures. What do the pictures add to the story?

The pictures tell more about Flag than the words do.

Content Connections

LISTENING/
SPEAKING

Persuade Me

small group

Help the girl find Flag! Make a lost-dog poster for Flag. Use your poster to persuade your classmates to search for Flag, too. Which poster is the most persuasive? Take a vote.

> **LOST DOG!**
>
> Please help find Flag!
> He's the best dog ever!
> If found, please call
> 555-5056.

MUSIC

Put Flag's Story to Music

large group

First, make up words to tell Flag's story. Think about his feelings during each part of the story. Then make a tape with different types of music to show his feelings. Play the tape as your group tells the story.

> I ran after a rabbit. It was a fun chase. I could tell it was going to be a great day!

Make a Food Chain

Internet

small group

Find out more about a desert animal. Is your animal a predator or is it prey? What does it eat? Take notes. Make a food chain. Explain the food chain to your group.

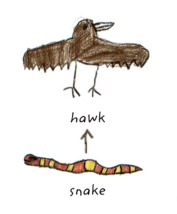

hawk

↑

snake

WRITING

Write to Tell How You Feel

on your own

Write something to tell how the story "Lost" made you feel. How did you feel at first? How did your feelings change as you read the story? Choose the best form:

- a journal entry
- a friendly letter.

Remember to use feeling words and to make your writing sound like you.

I felt worried when the girl and her dad could not find Flag.

Past Tense Verbs

Listen and sing.

Song

Rattlesnake and Jackrabbit

One day Rattlesnake slithered by

In the desert hot and dry.

Snake was hungry as could be.

He waited for Rabbit patiently.

He opened his mouth

when she appeared.

But Rabbit was quick.

She disappeared!

—*Jane Zion Brauer*

Tune: "Six Little Ducks"

How Language Works

A **verb** shows when an action happens.

Now	In the Past
1. The coyote **howls**.	The coyote **howled** last night.
2. A lizard **rests** in the sand.	Yesterday a lizard **rested** in the sand.
3. We **play** in the dunes.	Last week we **played** in the dunes.
4. The prospector **looks** for gold.	The prospector **looked** for gold long ago.
5. They **camp** in the canyon.	They **camped** in the canyon last summer.

Practice with a Partner

Make each red verb tell about the past. Then say the sentence.

visit   **1.** Last week I _____ the desert.

start   **2.** It _____ to rain.

wait   **3.** A mouse _____ in its hole.

disappear   **4.** A snake _____ under a rock.

climb   **5.** I _____ into the car!

Put It in Writing

Pretend that you took a trip to the desert with your family. Write about the things you saw and did. When you edit your work, make sure the verbs are correct.

A snake crawled after a mouse.

Show What You Know

Talk About Deserts

In this unit, you read a science article and a story about the desert. Look back at the unit. What was your favorite fact about the desert? Summarize it and tell your partner why you think it is interesting.

Make a Mind Map

Work with a partner. Make a mind map to show what you learned about deserts.

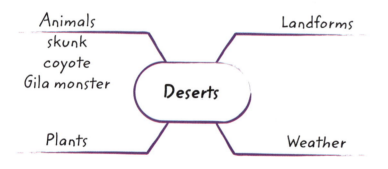

Think and Write

What is life in the desert like? Draw a picture and write a caption. Add this writing to your portfolio. Include work that shows what you learned about the desert.

Read and Learn More

Leveled Books

Explore!
by Janine Wheeler

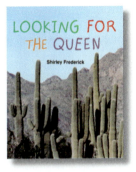

Looking for the Queen
by Shirley Frederick

Theme Library

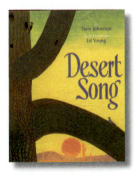

Desert Song
by Tony Johnston

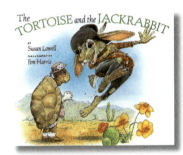

The Tortoise and the Jackrabbit
by Susan Lowell

Internet

Go to: www.hbavenues.com

Saguaro Cactus

Desert Animals

Desert Story

Eve Bunting's
WORLD OF STORIES

Make a Book

Work with your class to make a book.

1. One person completes the sentence:
   One time, not too long ago, ___ .
2. Each person adds a sentence.
3. Copy your sentence. Draw a picture.
4. Put the pages in a book.

Social Studies Words

United States Symbols

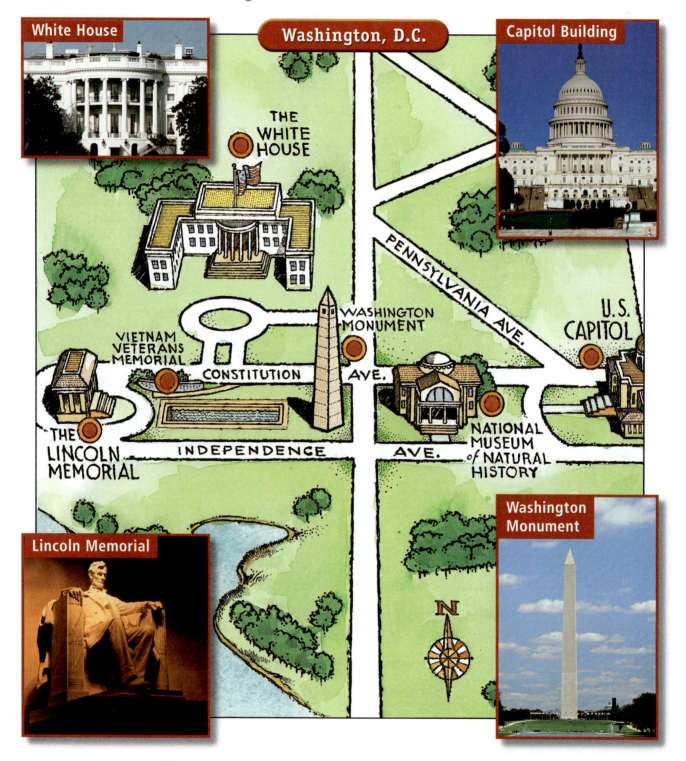

White House

Washington, D.C.

Capitol Building

THE WHITE HOUSE

PENNSYLVANIA AVE.

WASHINGTON MONUMENT

U.S. CAPITOL

VIETNAM VETERANS MEMORIAL

CONSTITUTION AVE.

THE LINCOLN MEMORIAL

INDEPENDENCE AVE.

NATIONAL MUSEUM of NATURAL HISTORY

N

Lincoln Memorial

Washington Monument

▼ Statue of Liberty

▲ U.S. Flag

▲ bald eagle

▲ Liberty Bell

299

Song

The Statue of Liberty

Statue of Liberty

We're taking a **journey**,
To an **island** so small,
Where a lady called Liberty
Stands graceful and tall.

Our thoughts are **respectful**,
For we **understand**,
She welcomes all **immigrants**
Who come to this land.

—*Maxine Schur*

Tune: "On Top of Old Smoky"

ferry

Key Words

Statue of Liberty

journey

island

respectful

understand

immigrant

ferry

A Picnic in October

by **Eve Bunting**

illustrated by **Nancy Carpenter**

Read a Story

Genre

This story tells about events that could really happen. It is <mark>realistic fiction</mark>. In the story, a boy and his family celebrate a birthday.

Characters

Tony

Grandma

Setting

This story happens in the New York Harbor in New York City.

New York City

💿 **Selection Reading**

1 Tony and his family have a picnic in October. Find out why.

Dad and Mom and I take the bus to Battery Park. We're carrying the stuff for the birthday picnic. Mom has the cake.

It's October 28, bright and sharp and cold. Really cold.

"Why do we always have to do this?" I ask Mom. "A picnic in October! It's dumb!"

"This is the way Grandma wants it," Mom says.

And that's the end of it.

When we get to Battery Park, I see Grandma right away. She's wearing her bright green coat. The wind **ruffles** the fake fur collar around her neck. Grandpa's with her, and Uncle Joe and Aunt Louise, and my cousins, Rosa and Mike. They're **loaded with** picnic stuff, too.

We all hug and kiss.

ruffles blows
loaded with carrying a lot of

Grandpa reaches inside his overcoat and gives Rosa and Mike and me **licorice sticks**. He keeps a row of them in his top jacket pocket the way other people keep pens. He's wearing his usual black hat. Rosa says he wears that hat to bed. But I don't think so.

licorice sticks pieces of candy

"We'd better hurry and get in the ==ferry== line,"
Aunt Louise says.

I look at the line, and I can see we're going
to have a long wait.

We stomp our feet and blow on our hands.

Across on the ==island==, the ==Statue of Liberty==
stands, bright and gleaming.

"She was **all spruced up** a few years back,"
Grandma says. "She sure looks good for her age."

all spruced up fixed and cleaned

Grandpa strokes Grandma's cheek. "Like you, sweetheart," he says. Grandpa can **be really soppy**.

Mike's holding the cake now, in its **see-through** container. "Remember last year? Remember trying to get all the candles to fit on here?"

I **nod**. "We only brought ten this time. Grandma says when you're really old, you don't care about having one for every year, anyway."

be really soppy show his feelings too much
see-through clear
nod move my head up and down to show "yes"

Before You Move On

1. **Character** Tell what Grandpa is like.

2. **Conclusion** Why does Tony think a picnic in October is a bad idea?

A woman with a thick braid of black hair pulls at my arm. She's wearing a long colored skirt that **brushes** the ground beneath her coat. There's a little girl with her and a man in loose white pants that **flap** in the wind. The woman tugs harder on my arm. She points to the ferry, which is **chugging** away from the **dock**. She's talking to me. I don't understand the words, but I can see she's worried.

"What's she saying?" Mike asks me.

"I think she's worried because the boat's gone," I say.

---

brushes touches
flap move back and forth
chugging moving slowly
dock place where you get on the boat

I smile at the woman. "It's OK," I say. "There'll be another boat." I point at the ferry, then at the end of the line, then back at the ferry. I make a turn-around sweep with my arm. "Another will come."

She smiles and nods. I can tell she **understands** and feels better.

Mike **sniggers**. "Man! You look like a third-base umpire, waving your arms like that. You are acting stupid."

"Don't be rude, Mike," Grandma says. "Tony was being kind. You are <u>not</u> being kind."

I wiggle my ears at Mike, and that makes him laugh. Grandma gives him another **disapproving stare**.

---

sniggers laughs
disapproving stare look so he will act better

The next ferry comes and we manage to
squeeze on. I watch for the woman and her
family, but they don't make it onto this boat. I
hope they don't give up.

The grown-ups rush inside where it's warm.
We just put our stuff in there and run to the front
of the boat.

Liberty Island is coming closer. The statue is
getting bigger.

---

squeeze on get on it

We **straggle off** at the dock, **lugging** the picnic stuff.

The island is crowded, but Dad finds a grassy spot. The grown-ups **spread the blankets**. The three of us run around.

"That's the Verrazano Bridge," I say.

Mike points. "There's Brooklyn." Brooklyn is where Mike and Rosa live.

Sailboats **dip into** the wind.

---

straggle off slowly get off
lugging carrying
spread the blankets put the blankets flat on the ground
dip into lean in

"There's Ellis Island," Rosa says **in a reading kind of way**. "Seventeen million <mark>immigrants</mark> entered the United States of America through Ellis Island. We learned that in school."

"You told us last year," I say.

Rosa's offended. "So?"

---

in a reading kind of way as if she is reading the words

Rosa's offended Rosa feels hurt

"Tony! Rosa! Mike!"
Dad calls.

"**Chow time**," Mike says.

We all sit on the blankets except for Grandma and Grandpa. We brought the folding chairs for them.

There's **a ton** of food.

Our paper plates keep blowing away. We try throwing them back, but the wind carries them in the other direction. We have to chase them again. We **dump them in the trash**. The **ginger ale** is so cold it burns my throat.

Chow time It is time to eat
a ton a lot
dump them in the trash throw them away
ginger ale soda

Before You Move On

1. **Details** How does Tony help the woman in line?

2. **Character** What is Tony like? What is Grandma like?

317

3 Find out why the Statue of Liberty is so special to Grandma.

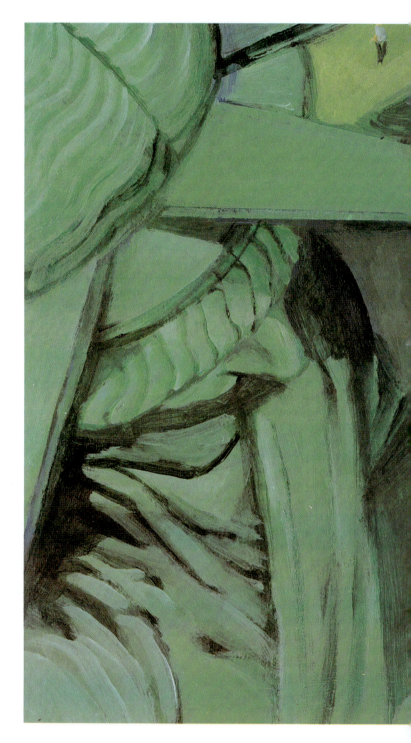

Lady Liberty gazes down on us with her calm, old eyes.

"You'd think she'd get tired, holding her arm up like that," Rosa says.

I groan. "Give us a break! She's not <u>real</u>!"

Grandma frowns. "She's not alive, if that's what you mean. But she's certainly real. And so is what she stands for."

She smiles at Grandpa. "It's time for the birthday. Light the candles, Luigi."

Lady Liberty The Statue of Liberty
I groan. "Give us a break! I make a noise and say "Stop joking!

The wind blows out every match Grandpa lights. The candles lean toward Staten Island and the **wicks** get stuck in the frosting. We straighten them and make a **hands barrier** between them and the wind.

It's a miracle they stay lit while Dad lifts the cake for Grandma to blow them out. **They go with one huff** when we take our hands away.

"*Brava, Bella!*" Grandpa cries. *Brava* means "you're wonderful" in Italian. *Bella* means "beautiful." Grandpa is being soppy again.

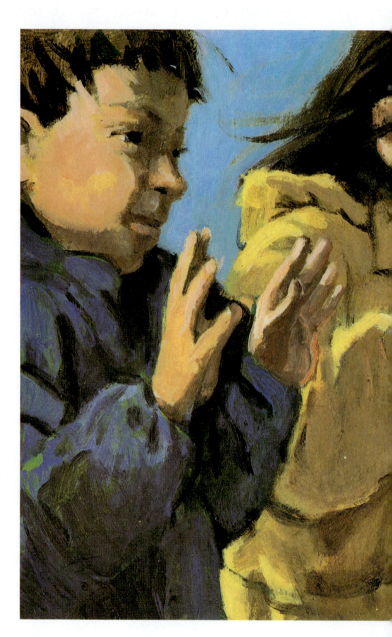

wicks top part of the candles
hands barrier wall with our hands
It's a miracle We are surprised
They go with one huff The candles go out all at once

Dad refills our paper cups, and we stand to face Lady Liberty. "Happy birthday!" we shout. We touch cups and drink.

"When I came from the **old country**," Grandma says, "I came out here, and I said: 'Thank you, Lady Liberty. Thank you for taking me in.' I spoke in Italian, of course, but she understands all languages. 'This is America, and I am here, and I am a part of it,' I thought."

She says this every time. Grandma thinks the statue is **such a big deal**.

---

old country country where I was born, Italy
such a big deal a very important thing

Grandpa leads us in the Happy Birthday song to Lady Liberty. Then Grandma begins to **recite** the famous words: *"Give me your tired, your poor, Your huddled masses yearning to breathe free . . . "*

There's more. She recites them here on Lady Liberty's birthday every single year. **Not much wonder** she knows them by heart. Rosa does, too. **She's very uppity about it**.

Grandma blows kisses, so we feel we have to. I **sincerely** hope no one is watching.

---

recite say aloud
Not much wonder It is not a surprise
She's very uppity about it She thinks she's better than us because of it
sincerely really

Before You Move On
1. **Character** How does Tony feel about the picnic? How do you know?
2. **Inference** Why did Grandma say thank you to Lady Liberty?

Tony changes how he feels about the statue. Why?

After that we pack up what's left of the picnic and walk to the back part of the island, called the mall. There's a **birthday program** there, too. A brass band is playing. The **Veterans of Foreign Wars** are having a parade. What a party Lady Liberty's having! We stay for a while, and then we come back around.

---

birthday program special event for Lady Liberty's birthday

Veterans of Foreign Wars group of people who fought in wars for the United States

I see the woman in her long, bright skirt with the man and the little girl.

I **grin**. "Look! There she is! They made it!" I say. "They got the ferry."

Grandma nods. "I bet they're new Americans. I know how they feel."

grin smile

They are **staring** up at the statue. Then the man says something. They hold hands and bow their heads. The way they stand, **so still**, so <mark>respectful</mark>, so . . . so peaceful, makes me **choke up**. Maybe they've come to the end of a long <mark>journey</mark>, farther than just from Battery Park to Liberty Island.

staring looking
so still without moving
choke up start to cry

I put my arm around Grandma and hold my cup of ginger ale up to Lady Liberty. I think I'm seeing her for the very first time.

"*Brava, Bella!*" I say. "Happy birthday!"

And I don't care who's watching.

Before You Move On

1. **Character** Tony sees the woman again. How does that change his feelings?

2. **Prediction** Do you think Tony will want to have a picnic next year? Why?

Nancy Carpenter

Nancy Carpenter started drawing as soon as she could hold a crayon. She liked to draw the things she saw when she traveled with her family.

Two of the books Ms. Carpenter has illustrated were written by Eve Bunting: *Tweenies* and *A Picnic in October*. *A Picnic in October* was a perfect job for Ms. Carpenter because she can see Ellis Island and the Statue of Liberty from her neighborhood. Finding details for her illustrations was just a ferry ride away!

Think and Respond

Strategy: Analyze Character

A character can change because of the people he or she knows and the events that happen. Make a character map for Tony. Think about how Tony changes and why.

Tony ← **Name the character.**

Tony's Thoughts and Feelings	People Tony Knows
page 305: thinks the picnic is dumb	• Dad and Mom
page 306:	
page 309:	

List thoughts and feelings in order.

Look to see if Tony changes.

Interview a Character

Pretend you are Tony. Have your partner ask you questions. Use your character map to help you answer. Then switch.

Talk It Over

1 **Personal Response** Are you like Tony? How? How are you different?

2 **Conclusion** Why is the Statue of Liberty important to immigrants to the United States?

3 **Judgments** Do you think Grandma feels strongly about the Statue of Liberty? Do other characters? Give examples from the story.

4 **Speculate** This story tells about the Statue of Liberty. How would a social studies article be different?

Compare Characters

Compare the girl in "The Ugly Vegetables" with Tony in "A Picnic in October." How did each change?

Content Connections

Compare Languages

on your own

Tony says, "Brava, Bella" to express his good wishes and thankfulness to the Statue of Liberty. How do you give good wishes in other languages? Ask your parents or look in a dictionary. Say the words for the class and name the language.

"Meilleurs souhaits" means "best wishes" in French.

ART

Make a Holiday Symbol

small group

The Statue of Liberty is an important symbol to Grandma, and so is its birthday. What is an important day for your family? Make or draw a symbol that shows something about that day. Tell your group about the symbol and why it is important.

▲ Day of the Dead candy

Learn About a Symbol

Internet

partners

Research the history of an American symbol. Write questions and then look on the Internet or in books. Draw a picture of the symbol and make a chart. Share what you learn with the class.

The Statue of Liberty

| When | Built in 1884
Arrived in the
United States in 1885 |
| Where | Built in France
Now on Liberty Island
in New York Harbor |

WRITING

Write a Guidebook

large group

Make a guide to welcome people to your city. You might tell them where to buy groceries, get a library card, or have fun. Include a map so they won't get lost! Display the guide in your visitors bureau.

Welcome to
Dearborn, Michigan

Places to Visit:
Arab American National Museum
Henry Ford Estate
Dearborn Ballet Theatre

Read Long Words

Some long words have a root word and a suffix. A
suffix is a word part that is added to the end of a word.
When you read a long word:

✔ Find word parts you know.
✔ Use the meaning of the word
part to help you figure out what
the whole word means.

Try the strategy.

Suffix	Example	Meaning
-ly	quickly	in a way that is quick
-or	editor	person who edits
-ful	thoughtful	full of thought

The Statue of Liberty

The Statue of Liberty stands proudly on
Liberty Island in New York Harbor. It was
a gift from France to the United States
more than one hundred years ago.

A French sculptor designed and built
the Statue in France. It was taken apart
and shipped to the United States in 350
pieces! Since 1886 "Lady Liberty" has
welcomed millions of thankful people
to America's shores.

I know what *thank* means. I also know that *-ful* means "full of." So *thankful* must mean "full of thanks."

Practice

Take this test and ==read long words==.

Read the article. Then read each item. Choose the best answer.

There are many things a <u>visitor</u> can do at the Statue of Liberty National Monument. Park guides will <u>gladly</u> give you a tour. There is a museum that tells about the Statue's history. You can visit the Statue's crown, too. Be <u>careful</u> when you climb the 354 steps! Then enjoy a beautiful view of New York City from the crown.

1 What does the word <u>visitor</u> mean?
- ⬭ full of visits
- ⬭ without visits
- ⬭ person who visits

2 What does the word <u>gladly</u> mean?
- ⬭ not glad
- ⬭ often glad
- ⬭ in a way that is glad

3 What does the word <u>careful</u> mean?
- ⬭ without care
- ⬭ full of care
- ⬭ often caring

Respectfully Yours,
EVE BUNTING

Tell Me About Yourself

Think about a time you moved to a new place.
Ask and answer these questions with your partner.

1. Were you **homesick** for your old home
   after you moved?

2. Was it difficult to **start over** in a new place?

3. What are your favorite **memories** of your
   old home?

4. What is your favorite **experience** in your
   new home?

5. How do you **connect** your life here with
   your life in your old home?

6. The Statue of Liberty is a **symbol** for immigrants.
   What symbol would you choose for your new place?

Read an Interview

In an **interview**, one person asks another person questions to get information. When you read an interview, look for the **questions** and the **answers**.

question — **Mrs. Schur:** Was it hard to leave Ireland? Why did your family leave?

answer — **Mrs. Bunting:** I was an only child, so it was very hard to leave my mother behind.

Selection Reading

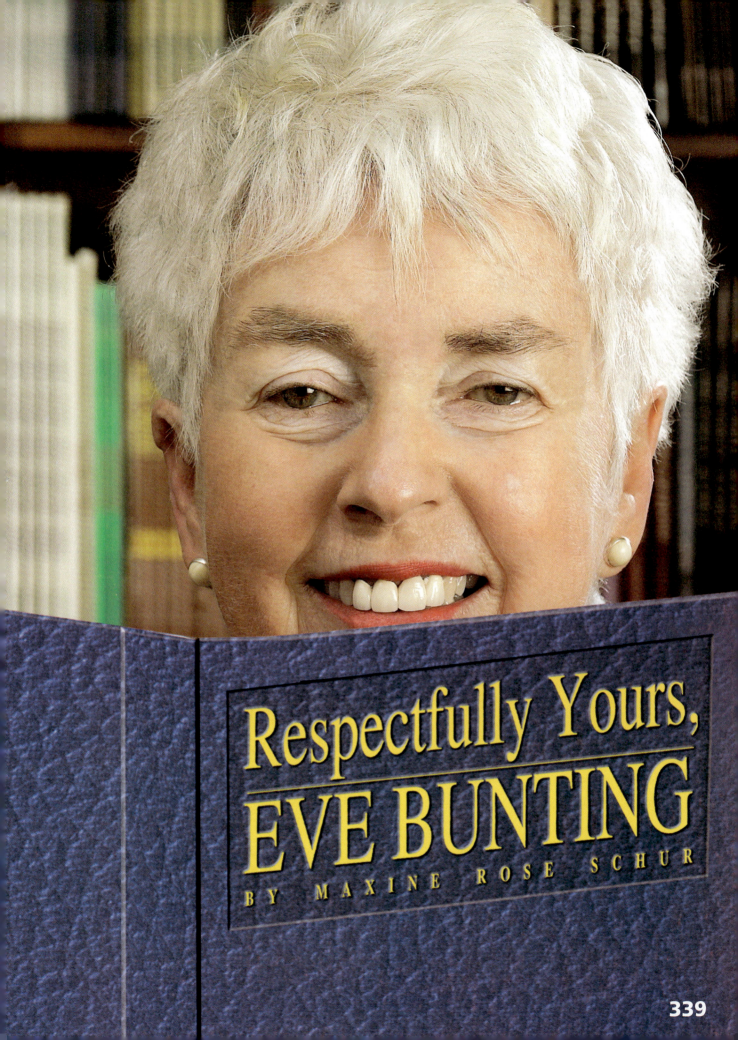

Respectfully Yours, EVE BUNTING

BY MAXINE ROSE SCHUR

Set Your Purpose

Find out about
Eve Bunting's life.
What happens?
Why?

Eve Bunting is the author of more
than 150 books, including *A Picnic in
October*. In this interview, Maxine
Rose Schur asks her about her life
and her writing.

▲ Eve Bunting and her father in her
hometown, Maghera, Ireland

Mrs. Schur: Why did you
become a writer?

Mrs. Bunting: I think I always
wanted to be a writer. When
I was a little girl, I would sit
with my father as he read
poetry to me. He was a
farmer **with the heart of
a poet**.

I didn't always understand the
meaning of the poems, but I
understood their sound. I
loved the sound of the words.
I wanted to put my own
words together to make them
beautiful, so I began to write
poems and stories just for fun.

---

with the heart of a poet who thought
like a person who writes poems

340

Mrs. Schur: Why did you start writing books?

Mrs. Bunting: When I moved to America from Ireland, I was lonely for a while. After a few years, I took a writing class. Through my stories I could share something about myself. They showed people what I <u>cared</u> about.

Writing became important to me. I made new friends with other writers, and I received wonderful letters from my readers. Writing **connects** me with so many people!

▲ Eve Bunting, center, with her family in Maxim, California

Before You Move On

1. **Cause/Effect** What did Mrs. Bunting's father do? How did this help her become a writer?

2. **Details** What do Mrs. Bunting's stories show people?

341

▲ Eve Bunting visits her hometown in Ireland.

Mrs. Schur: Was it hard to leave Ireland? Why did your family leave?

Mrs. Bunting: I was an only child, so it was very hard to leave my mother behind. We had **relatives** in the United States, and they told us there were a lot of jobs here.

Also, we thought of America as a magical land, like in the movies. We thought it would always be sunny, but I soon learned parts of America could be colder than Ireland!

---

relatives family members

342

▲ Eve Bunting, center, with her family in California

Before You Move On

1. **Cause/Effect** Why did Mrs. Bunting's family want to move to the United States?

2. **Inference** Why does Mrs. Bunting like to visit Ireland?

343

▲ Eve Bunting meets thousands of children every year.
Many, like her, are immigrants to the United States.

Mrs. Schur: Why are many of your books about
immigrants?

Mrs. Bunting: My own <mark>experience</mark> as an immigrant
led me to write books about other immigrants.

I wanted to show how hard it can be to <mark>start over</mark>
in a new country. I also wanted to show the good
things that can happen here.

▲ Eve Bunting signs books and talks with students.

Mrs. Schur: What would you tell a new immigrant?

Mrs. Bunting: Don't expect your life to be wonderful at first. Life in America is not like life in American movies. It's different. You may think your clothes look wrong. Your family may have to work very hard to make money, and you will feel lonely and <mark>homesick</mark>. Even if you speak English, you can feel this way.

Try to understand your new country. **Be open** and <u>work</u> at it. After a while you will make friends. Slowly, you will feel that you are part of America, too.

Be open Try new things

Before You Move On

1. **Conclusion** Why can life be hard for a new immigrant?

2. **Opinion** Do you agree with Mrs. Bunting about life in America? Why or why not?

Mrs. Schur: Where do you get your ideas for your books?

Mrs. Bunting: Sometimes people tell me stories that I turn into books. It's just like being given a gift!

Once, I was having lunch with some book sellers. One of them leaned across the table and whispered to me, "I own an olive tree in Greece." She told me that her grandfather had planted the tree for her so she would always have "a little bit of Greece." I loved this idea and turned it into my story, *I Have an Olive Tree*.

▼ Eve Bunting's edited draft of *I Have an Olive Tree*.

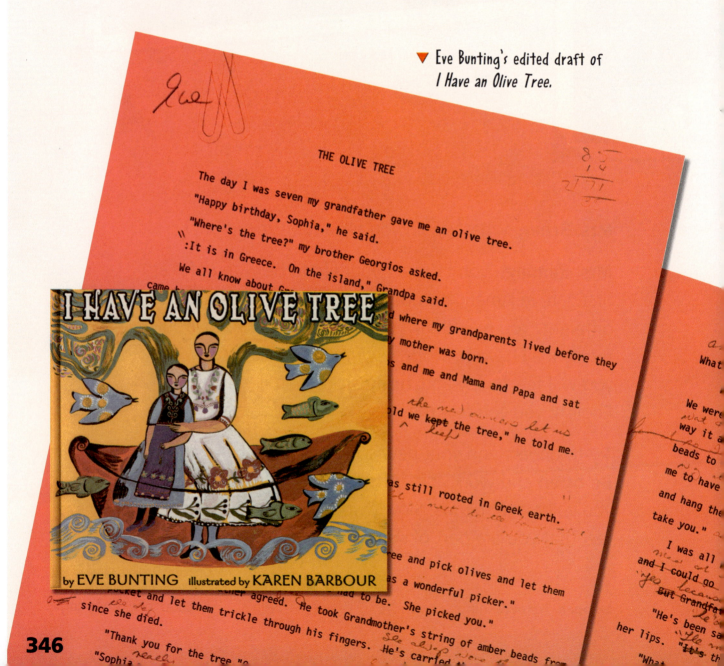

THE OLIVE TREE

The day I was seven my grandfather gave me an olive tree.

"Happy birthday, Sophia," he said.

"Where's the tree?" my brother Georgios asked.

":It is in Greece. On the island," Grandpa said.

We all know about G

where my grandparents lived before they

mother was born.

s and me and Mama and Papa and sat

ld we kept the tree," he told me.

as still rooted in Greek earth.

ee and pick olives and let them

as a wonderful picker." She picked you."

Mrs. Schur: How did you get the idea to write *Dreaming of America*?

Mrs. Bunting: An editor asked me to write about a girl named Annie Moore. At first, I wasn't interested in writing about her because I had never heard of her. When I began to read about Annie Moore, though, my feelings changed. I **admired** this strong little girl.

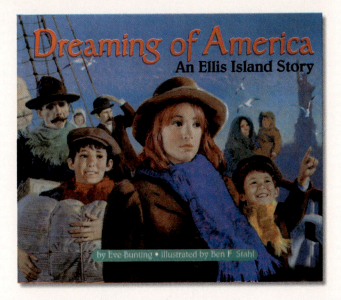

Annie Moore came to America without her parents and had to take care of her two younger brothers. As an immigrant myself, I could understand her **courage** and her fears. So, I decided to let others know about her.

An editor A person who edits books
admired liked
courage bravery

it for?
andfather died when I was in the third grade and I cried and cried.
with him around his bed and I got to hold his hand. It felt the
did, dry and rough and knotty. My mother had given him Grandmother's
and he crumpled them up and gave them to me. At first I thought he wanted
m, as a keepsake. But he said: :Sophia, will you go to the island
the olive tree, for your Grandmother and me? Your mother will
led up and sniffly but I nodded although I wasn't sure how
reece, so far away. And just to do this. Mama
had left more than two thousand
and saving," Ma

2

Before You Move On

1. **Details** Tell two ways Mrs. Bunting gets ideas for her books.

2. **Cause/Effect** Why did Mrs. Bunting change her mind about Annie Moore?

Mrs. Schur: What gave you the idea for *Going Home*?

Mrs. Bunting: Once, when my husband and I were driving through the Central Valley of California, I saw hundreds of workers picking the crops. It was hot, and I felt badly for them. I decided I wanted to do a book about these migrant workers. I asked the **boss** if I could talk to them. He told me to come back in the evening. I did.

The workers told me they **gave up** their life in Mexico to give their children a better life in the United States. Their biggest wish was to return to Mexico at Christmas to give nice presents to their families. That became the story *Going Home*.

---

boss person in charge
gave up left

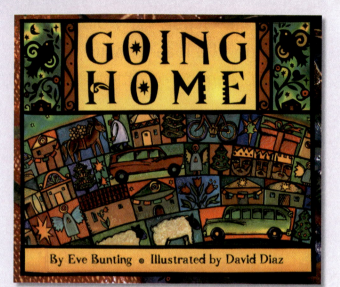

GOING HOME

By Eve Bunting • Illustrated by David Diaz

He gives me my

buy?"

"You're not to

Day you were sicker

"I never buy th

my porridge fast. My

stall at nine. He's

Market Day

by Eve Bu

illustrat

(Page 2—

farmers, tink

dedication wi

(Pages

The fi

Soon a

Mrs. Schur: *Market Day* is about Ireland. Why did you write this story?

Mrs. Bunting: When you are an immigrant, you never forget where you came from. One of my favorite <mark>memories</mark> is of market day.

Our town had a market day every week. It was like a **fair**. I could buy all sorts of **sweet treats** for just a penny. I loved to look at all the colorful things for sale and to see all my friends. My memories of market day are still part of who I am.

---

fair big celebration
sweet treats candies

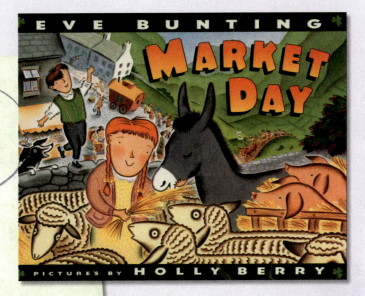

printout of final MS for reference.

ng

by Holly Berry

Map of roads leading to main square of town—with
, gypsies, etc. on their way. Copyright and
be incorporated as signage.)

)

Thursday of every month is Market Day.

waken, I rush downstairs. My father is already
eakfast. He gives me the top of his two boiled eggs.
hen a hen's in love her

Before You Move On

1. **Cause/Effect** Why did Mrs. Bunting write *Going Home*?

2. **Personal Experience** What are your favorite memories of home?

349

Mrs. Schur: What do you most like to write about?

Mrs. Bunting: My books always show how important it is to **treat others with respect** and to be kind.

A Day's Work is an example. It's based on a true story. My son had a big **landscaping** job, and he hired a Mexican man to help him for the day. My son had already planted 300 plants. He asked the man to pull all the weeds around the plants, but the man did not understand English well. He pulled all the plants and left the weeds.

---

treat others with respect be nice to other people
landscaping gardening

At the end of the day, my son saw what the man did. When my son told the man that he had made a big mistake, the man said that he would work the next day for free. He would replant all the 300 plants and pull the weeds, too! My son admired the man's wish to do the job right, so he paid him for a second day. My son began to respect this man very much for his honesty.

Before You Move On

1. **Details** What do Mrs. Bunting's books always show about people?

2. **Paraphrase** Tell the true story about Mrs. Bunting's son.

Mrs. Schur: Why do you use <mark>symbols</mark> in your stories?

Mrs. Bunting: Some things are easier to write about as symbols than to write about them directly. Before I immigrated to America, I came here on a vacation. We arrived on a boat.

On a gray morning, we all rushed **on deck** to see the Statue of Liberty. I will never, ever, forget it. I saw many immigrants. I saw that they were **thrilled** because of what the statue <u>meant</u> to them: a life that is fair and free.

In *A Picnic in October*, the Statue of Liberty is a symbol to all immigrants of America's promise for a better life.

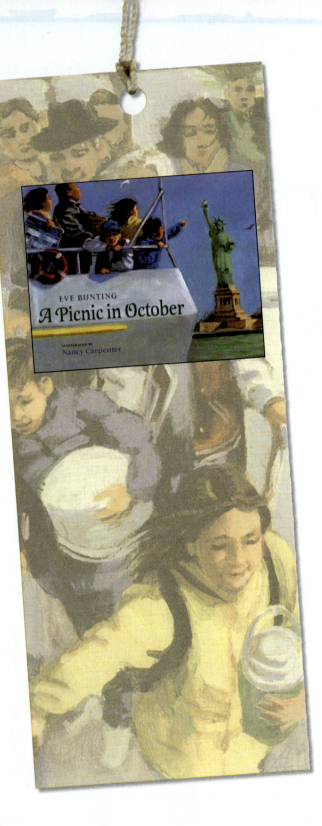

EVE BUNTING
A Picnic in October
ILLUSTRATED BY
Nancy Carpenter

---

on deck to the top floor of the boat
thrilled very happy

▲ Eve Bunting loves to talk about her stories with children.

Mrs. Schur: You have written so many books. Is there one book that is your favorite?

Mrs. Bunting: I like to write for every child, for every age, and for every interest. I couldn't possibly choose just one book. I love them all!

Before You Move On

1. **Summary** Tell about when Mrs. Bunting first visited America.

2. **Cause/Effect** Why does Mrs. Bunting write so many books?

Think and Respond

Strategy: Cause and Effect

Some kinds of writing tell what happens and why it happens. Make a cause-and-effect chart. Tell about Mrs. Bunting's life.

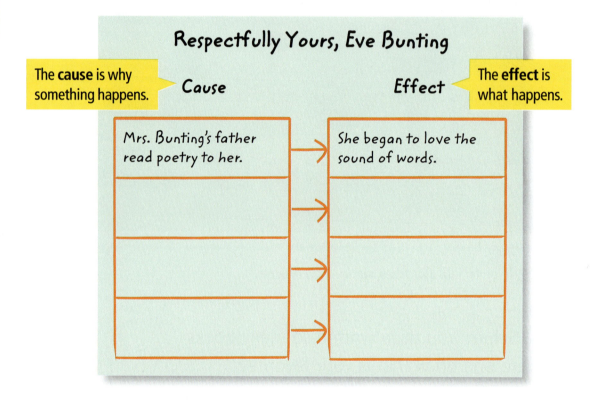

Respectfully Yours, Eve Bunting

The **cause** is why something happens.

Cause

Effect

The **effect** is what happens.

Cause	Effect
Mrs. Bunting's father read poetry to her.	She began to love the sound of words.

Draw Conclusions

Think about Mrs. Bunting's life. Draw conclusions about how the events changed her life.

Talk It Over

1 **Personal Response** Would you like to read more books by Mrs. Bunting? Why?

2 **Conclusion** Mrs. Bunting cares a lot about children and their families. How do you know?

3 **Speculate** Think about stories you know. Which story do you think Mrs. Bunting might like? Why?

4 **Personal Experience** Tell about a time when you were inspired to write a story or draw a picture.

Compare Texts

Compare the interview with the biography on page 329. How are they different? How are they alike?

The interview feels more personal. The person is talking to me.

Content Connections

MATH

Make a Human Graph

large group

Make a bar graph to show where your classmates were born. Ask everyone born in the same country to line up together. Count the people in each line. Graph the information. Write sentences to explain the data. Share them with a partner.

Five kids came from Mexico, but two were born in the U.S.

SOCIAL STUDIES

Tell an Immigrant's Story

small group

Internet

A Chinese boy and his family came to San Francisco.

Find a historic photo of an immigrant family. Tell a story about the photo. Practice the story with your group. Switch groups. Share the photo and story with your new group.

Make a Passport

large group

1. Put pages together to make a passport.

2. Design a stamp that tells about you.

3. "Visit" your classmates. Ask them questions and write what you learn. Collect their stamps for your passport.

I visited
Juan in Cuba

and I found out
He likes black beans and rice. He also likes football.

WRITING

Write to Give Information

on your own

Write about how Eve Bunting gets her ideas. Choose the best form:

- a summary
- an article.

Try to use correct spelling, capitalization, punctuation, and grammar.

Eve Bunting gets the ideas for her books from many places. A book seller told her a story that became "I Have an Olive Tree."

Past Tense Verbs

Listen and sing.

Song

In the U.S.A!

I left my native land.

I made a trip across the sea.

I felt alone, but you

Held out your hand to me.

You talked and laughed with me.

You were a friend to me.

That was how I learned to love

My home in this country.

—*Jane Zion Brauer*

Tune: "Early One Morning"

How Language Works

Some **verbs** have special forms for the **past tense**.

Verb	In the Past	Examples:
take	took	Yesterday we **took** a ferry ride.
give	gave	I **gave** the man my ticket.
go	went	We **went** to Liberty Island.
see	saw	We **saw** the Statue of Liberty.
say	said	"It's beautiful!" I **said**.
have	had	We **had** a picnic on the island.
come	came	Then we **came** back to the city.
is	was	It **was** a great day!

Practice with a Partner

Make each red verb tell about the past. Then say the sentence.

come   1. My family _____ to America last year.

give   2. Our cousins _____ us a big welcome.

take   3. They _____ us to their apartment.

see   4. We _____ many new things.

say   5. Mom _____, "I already feel as if I am home."

Put It in Writing

Think of a special place in America. Write about a real or pretend visit there. Tell what you saw and did. When you edit your work, make sure the verbs are in the correct tense.

We went to the White House. I saw pictures of the presidents.

Show What You Know

Talk About the Author

In this unit, you read a story and an interview with Eve Bunting. Look back at this unit. What is the most surprising thing you learned about being a writer? Why do you think it is surprising? Share with your group.

Make a Mind Map

Work with a partner. Make a mind map to show how a writer gets ideas for new stories.

- personal experiences and memories
- other people's stories
- How a writer gets ideas
- a book seller's olive tree
- family experiences
- assignments

Think and Write

What did you learn about Eve Bunting? Write a paragraph. Add it to your portfolio. Also include work that shows what you learned about being an author.

Read and Learn More

Leveled Books

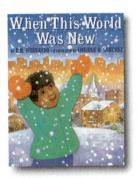

When This World Was New
by D.H. Figueredo

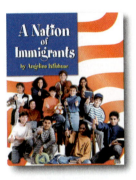

A Nation of Immigrants
by Guadalupe Lopez

Theme Library

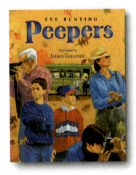

Peepers
by Eve Bunting

Gleam and Glow
by Eve Bunting

Internet

Go to: www.hbavenues.com

U.S. Symbols

Say Hello

U.S. Immigration

Good for You!

Choose Foods to Eat

1. Work with a partner. Draw something you like to eat.
2. Explain your food to the class.

3. Then put everyone's drawings together. Choose different foods to put on your plate.
4. Tell why you chose each food.

Take Care of Your Body

Eat Healthy Foods Every Day

Fats, oils, and sweets
Eat very few.

Milk, yogurt, and cheese
2–3 servings

Meat, poultry, fish, beans, eggs, and nuts
2–3 servings

Vegetables
3–5 servings

Fruits
2–4 servings

Breads, cereals, rice, and pasta
6–11 servings

Get Exercise

▲ Exercise builds a strong heart and lungs.

Get Rest

▲ Sleep is the best way to rest your body.

Keep Clean

▲ Keep your body clean. Brush your teeth every day.

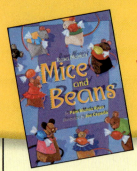

Vocabulary

Song

Rosa María **prepared** every day
For the fiesta just one week away.
The **meal** was **important**.
The **menu** was nice.
She made enchiladas
And lemonade on ice.

She thought all was ready.
How did she **forget**
To fill the piñata?
She was so upset!

Tune: "Arroz con leche" (Rice with Milk)

Key Words

prepare

meal

important

menu

forget

helpful

possible

remember

But her **helpful** friends
Made it **possible**
For the children to play
Because they **remembered**
To fill the piñata that day.

—Maria Del Rey

Rosa María's

Mice
and
Beans

by **Pam Muñoz Ryan**

illustrated by **Joe Cepeda**

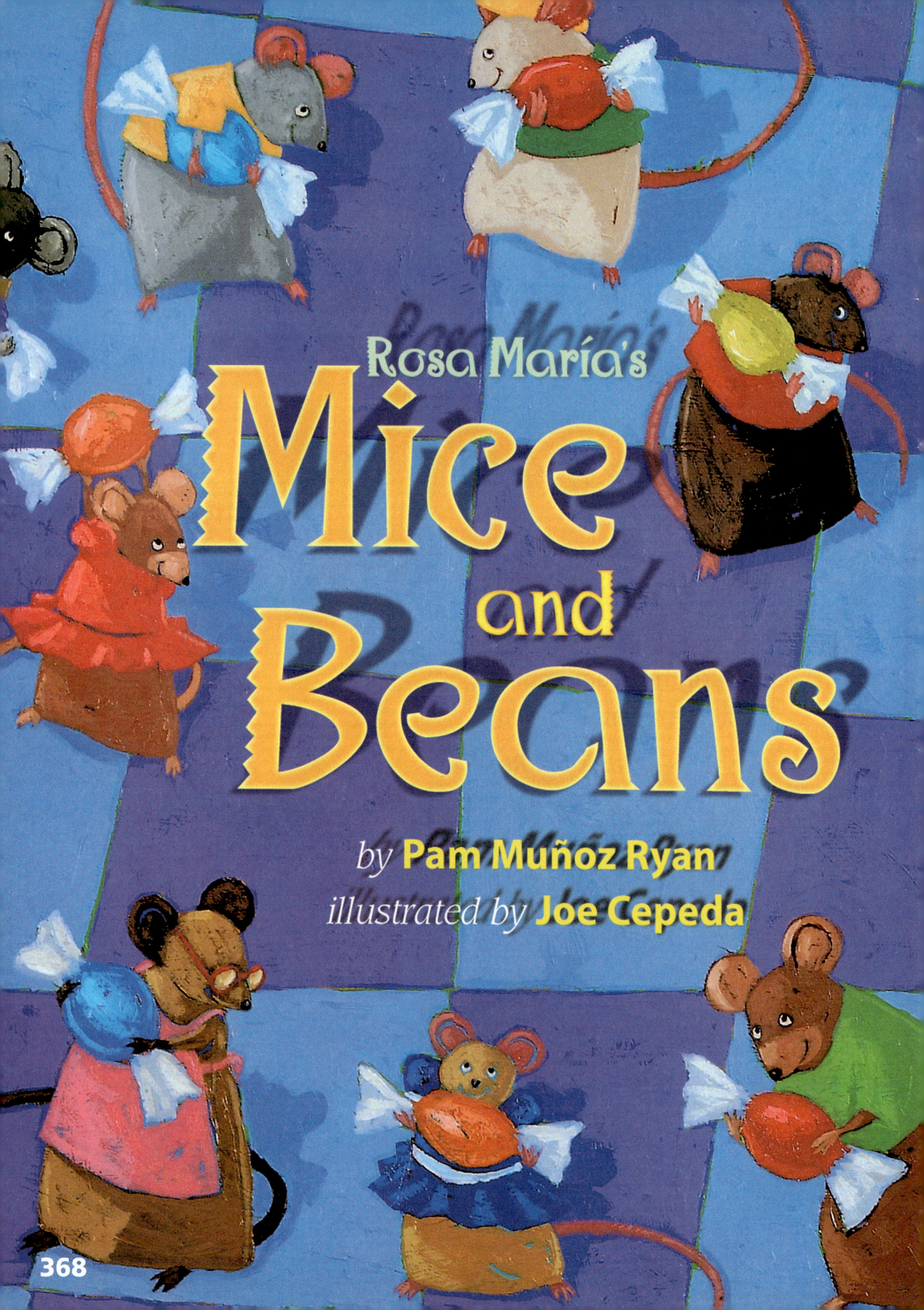

Read a Fantasy

Genre

A **fantasy** tells about events that couldn't happen in real life. This story is about how some mice help Rosa María prepare for a birthday party.

Characters

Rosa María

mice

Setting

This story happens in Rosa María's house.

Selection Reading

1

Rosa María wants to have a party. How does she prepare for it?

Rosa María lived in a tiny house with a tiny yard. But she **had a big heart, a big family**, and more than anything, she loved to cook big <mark>meals</mark> for them.

In one week, her youngest grandchild, Little Catalina, would be seven years old, and the whole family would squeeze into her *casita* for the party.

---

had a big heart, a big family was very kind and had a big family

casita small house (in Spanish)

Rosa María didn't mind because she believed what her mother had always said: **"When there's room in the heart, there's room in the house**, except for a mouse."

When there's room in the heart, there's room in the house There is always enough space in the house for everyone you love

Sunday, Rosa María planned the **menu**: enchiladas, rice and beans (no dinner was complete without rice and beans!), birthday cake, lemonade, and a piñata filled with candy.

She ordered the birthday present. It was something Little Catalina had wanted for a long time.

Satisfied with the plans, she wiped down the table so she wouldn't get mice and took out a mousetrap just in case. She was sure she had set one the night before, but now she couldn't find it. Maybe she'd forgotten.

When it was set and ready to snap, she turned off the light and went to bed.

Satisfied Happy

Monday, Rosa María did the laundry. She washed and ironed her largest tablecloth and the twenty-four napkins that matched. But when she finished, she only counted twenty-three.

"**No importa**," she said. "It doesn't matter. So what if someone has a napkin that doesn't match? The **important** thing is that we're all together."

After dinner she swept the floor and checked the mousetrap. But it was missing.

"Didn't I set one last night?" she wondered.

She hurried to the cupboard to **fetch** another. When it was set and ready to snap, she turned off the light and went to bed.

No importa It doesn't matter (in Spanish)
fetch get

Tuesday, Rosa María walked to the market. She filled her big **bolsa** with tortillas, cheese, red sauce, white rice, pinto beans, and a bag of candy. She bought a piñata. On her way home she stopped at the **pastelería** to order the cake.

After dinner, she washed the dishes and checked the mousetrap.

But it had **vanished**.

"**¡Qué boba soy!** Silly me, I must have forgotten, again!"

She hurried to the cupboard to fetch another. When it was set and ready to snap, she turned off the light and went to bed.

bolsa bag (in Spanish)
pastelería bakery (in Spanish)
vanished disappeared
¡Qué boba soy! Silly me! (in Spanish)

Before You Move On

1. **Paraphrase** Tell what Rosa María does to prepare for the party. Tell what the mice do.

2. **Inference** What happens to the mousetraps?

Things are
missing.
What does
Rosa María
do?

Wednesday, Rosa María
prepared the enchiladas. She dipped
the tortillas in red sauce, filled them
with cheese, and rolled them into fat
little **bundles**. She noticed the piñata
was missing a few feathers.

"*No importa*," she said. "Those
feathers won't make a difference to
the children when the piñata is filled
with candy."

---

bundles tubes

After dinner she **mopped up** the sauce and checked the mousetrap.

But it was gone again!

"I am so busy that I'm forgetting to remember!" she cried.

She hurried to the cupboard to fetch another. When it was set and ready to snap, she turned off the light and went to bed.

---

mopped up cleaned up

Thursday, Rosa María **simmered** the beans. She searched for her favorite wooden spoon, the one she always used to cook *frijoles*, but she couldn't find it.

"*No importa*," she said. "The beans will taste just as good if I use another spoon."

She added water all day long until the beans were **plump** and soft. Then she **scrubbed** the stove and checked the mousetrap.

But it was nowhere in sight!

"*¡Cielos!*" she said. "Heavens! Where is my mind?"

She hurried to the cupboard to fetch another. When it was set and ready to snap, she turned off the light and went to bed.

---

simmered slowly cooked
frijoles beans (in Spanish)
plump fat
scrubbed cleaned
¡Cielos! Heavens! (in Spanish)

Friday, Rosa María picked up the cake and seven candles. But she hadn't been able to find her big *bolsa* before she left.

"*No importa*," she said. "I'll carry the cake in one hand and the candles in the other."

Tomorrow was **the big day**. Rosa María knew she mustn't **forget** anything, so she carefully went over the list one last time.

---

the big day Little Catalina's birthday

After dinner she wrapped the cake and checked the mousetrap.

She couldn't believe her eyes.

No mousetrap!

"Thank goodness I've got **plenty**!"

She hurried to the cupboard to fetch another. When it was set and ready to snap, she turned off the light and went to bed.

---

plenty a lot of them

Saturday, Rosa María cooked the rice. As the workers **assembled** Little Catalina's present, she **set the table** and squeezed the juiciest lemons from her tree.

---

assembled built
set the table put everything on the table

"Let's see," she said, feeling very proud. "Enchiladas, rice and beans (no dinner was complete without rice and beans!), birthday cake, and lemonade. I know I have forgotten something, but what? The candles!"

But she only counted six.

"*No importa*," she said. "I will **arrange** the six candles in the shape of a seven, and Little Catalina will be just as happy. Now, everything is ready."

---

arrange put

Before You Move On

1. **Fantasy** What could really happen on pages 378–385? What couldn't?

2. **Comparison** Tell what the mice do while Rosa María cooks.

3 It is time for the party. What do you think will happen?

*B*ut WAS everything ready?

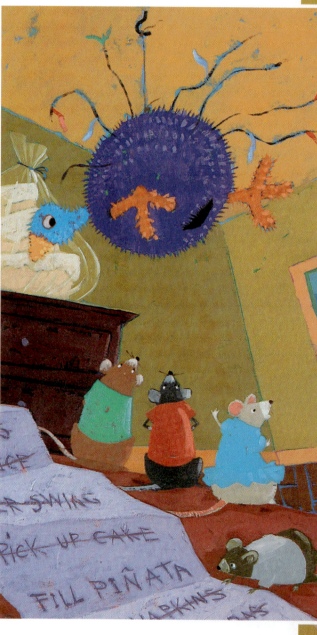

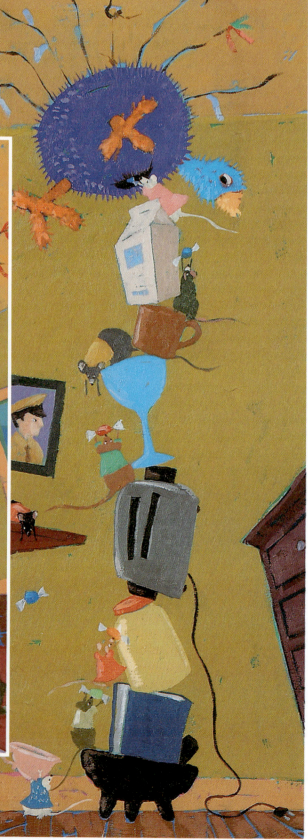

386

That afternoon Rosa María's family filled her tiny *casita*.

They ate the enchiladas and the rice and beans. They drank the fresh-squeezed lemonade. And they **devoured** the cake.

Little Catalina loved her present. It was a swing set! And after every cousin had a turn, they **chanted**, "*¡La piñata! ¡La piñata!*"

They ran to the walnut tree and threw a rope over a high branch.

---

devoured quickly ate
chanted said again and again

Whack! Whack! Little Catalina swung the piñata stick.

"Wait!" cried Rosa María as she remembered what she had forgotten. But it was too late.

Crack! The piñata **separated**, and the children **scrambled** to collect the candy.

---

separated broke
scrambled ran

"How could that be?" Rosa María **puzzled**. "I must have filled it without even **realizing**!"

She laughed at her own forgetfulness as she hugged her granddaughter and said, "*Feliz cumpleaños*, my Little Catalina. Happy birthday."

---

puzzled wondered
realizing knowing that I did it
Feliz cumpleaños Happy birthday (in Spanish)

After everyone had gone, Rosa María **tidied** her kitchen and thought **contentedly** about the *fiesta*. She pictured the happy look on Little Catalina's face when the candy spilled from the piñata. But Rosa María still couldn't remember when she had filled it. "*No importa*," she said. "It was a wonderful day."

tidied cleaned
contentedly happily
fiesta party (in Spanish)

But as Rosa María swept out the cupboard, she **discovered the telltale signs of mice**!

"¡*Ratones!*" she cried. "Where are my mousetraps? I will set them all!"

She **inched** to the floor and when she did, something caught her eye.

She looked closer.

"Maybe I didn't fill the piñata," she thought.

---

discovered the telltale signs of mice saw that mice had been there

¡***Ratones!*** Mice! (in Spanish)

inched moved slowly

"Was it **possible**?" she asked, shaking her head. "Could I have had help?"

Rosa María looked at the **leftovers**. Too much for one person.

And what was it her mother had always said? "When there's room in the heart, there's room in the house . . . even for a mouse."

"*¡Fíjate!* Imagine that!" she said. "I remembered the words wrong all these years."

Besides, how many could there be? Two? Four?

"*No importa*," she said. "It doesn't matter if a few **helpful** mice live here, too."

Then she turned off the light and went to bed . . .

---

leftovers food the family did not eat at the party
¡Fíjate! Imagine that! (in Spanish)

. . . and never set another mousetrap again.

Before You Move On

1. **Comparison** Compare the mouse fiesta with Rosa María's fiesta.

2. **Opinion** Will the mice help Rosa María again? Why or why not?

395

Meet the Author

Pam Muñoz Ryan

Pam Muñoz Ryan has happy memories of parties at her grandmother's little house. She says the family in *Mice and Beans* is "very similar to the big, noisy family gatherings that I grew up with."

Ms. Ryan's grandmother spoke only Spanish to her, so she learned the language when she was young. She uses both English and Spanish in her writing to show the joy and warmth of her family and to bring her characters to life.

Meet the Illustrator

Joe Cepeda

Joe Cepeda also remembers the wonderful birthday parties at his house. "There were always enchiladas, rice and beans, and a piñata. And lots of bruises, too, from diving for the fallen candy."

Today Mr. Cepeda still has birthday fiestas with his own family. He added a new tradition, though: a special hand-painted stick just for hitting the piñata.

Think and Respond

Strategy: Make Comparisons

Compare what Rosa María does with what the mice do. Make a chart.

Rosa María's Mice and Beans

Rosa María	Mice
1. planned a menu	1. made a list
2. washed and ironed the napkins	2. took a napkin

How does knowing what Rosa María and the mice do help you understand this story?

Identify Fantasy and Reality

Look at your chart. Talk about the characters' actions. Which actions could happen in real life? Which actions are fantasy?

Talk It Over

1 **Personal Response** Which part of the story did you like best? Why?

2 **Character** Do you think Rosa María was forgetful? Tell why or why not. Give examples.

3 **Conclusion** What do you think is the message of this story? Why?

4 **Personal Experience** Has someone ever helped you do something? Tell how the person helped.

Compare Artists' Styles

Look at the pictures in "Rosa María's Mice and Beans" and "Lost." How do the pictures make you feel?

Content Connections

large group

Act Out a Dinner Party

Pretend you are a famous person at a party with other guests. Talk and listen to the other guests. Act as if you are that person.

Hello, Mrs. Bunting. I'm James Ale. I'm glad you could come this evening.

partners

Use the Food Pyramid

Was Rosa María's fiesta meal healthy? Use the Food Pyramid on page 364 to find out. Discuss your conclusion with your partner.

Celebrate Celebrations

Internet

small group

Brainstorm celebrations, and then research one. Find out about its history, food, games, decorations, stories, music, and dances. Share what you learn with the class.

During Tet, people decorate their homes with kumquat trees.

WRITING

Write a Letter

partners

Pretend you are Rosa María. Write an apology letter to the mice. Give it to a partner. Your partner writes back to accept the apology.

July 17, 2004

Dear Mice,

  I am sorry I tried to catch you. I won't do that again.

Identify Main Idea and Details

The **main idea** is the most important idea of a story or article. **Details** give more information about the main idea. To identify the main idea and details:

✔ Read carefully.
✔ Think about the most important idea.
✔ Look for details that tell more about the main idea.

Try the strategy.

A HEALTHY PARTY MENU

Most of the food at birthday parties is sweet and full of fat. Why not plan a healthy party instead?

Here is how you can do it. Don't drink soda. Have fruit juice instead. Don't eat regular birthday cake. Try a dessert made with frozen yogurt. Replace potato chips with unbuttered popcorn or fruit. These party foods will be better for you and your guests.

The main idea is you can have a healthy party menu. One detail is that fruit is healthier than potato chips.

Practice

Take this test and **identify the main idea and details**.

Read the article. Then read each item. Choose the best answer.

The Food Guide Pyramid, created by the U.S. government in 1992, helps people plan healthy meals. The Pyramid has five food groups. For a healthy body, you need to eat foods from each group every day. The Pyramid suggests how much food to eat. People who are young and active need to eat the most food from each group.

1 What is the main idea of the article?

- ⬭ You should buy and eat healthy food.
- ⬭ When you are young, you need to exercise and eat healthy food.
- ⬭ The Food Guide Pyramid helps people plan healthy meals.
- ⬭ The Food Guide Pyramid tells you what foods to eat to have a healthy body.

✔ **Test Strategy**

Try to answer the question without reading the answer choices. Then compare your answer to the choices.

2 Which of these details can be added to the paragraph to go with the main idea?

- ⬭ Oils and sweets taste very good.
- ⬭ Many people don't use the Pyramid.
- ⬭ If you eat according to the Pyramid, you will not be healthy.
- ⬭ At the base of the Pyramid are starchy foods like breads and pasta.

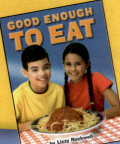

Ask Dr. Rinosa

Dear Dr. Rinosa,

Where does my **energy** come from?
—Ana

Dear Ana,

Energy comes from the food you eat! The amount of energy food gives you is measured in **calories**.

If you have a **diet** full of good foods, you will have a lot of energy.

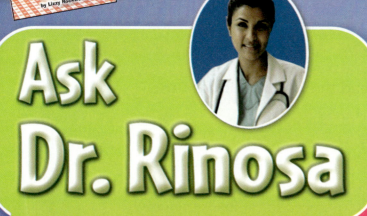

Dear Dr. Rinosa,
What are **nutrients**?
How does my body get them?
—Chan

Dear Chan,

Nutrients are the things your body needs to work. **Healthy** foods, like fruits and vegetables, **supply** your body with nutrients.

After you swallow the food, your body **absorbs** the nutrients. This is called **digestion**.

Read a Science Article

A **science article** is nonfiction. It can tell you about things that happen in nature.

✔ Look for **charts**. They organize important facts.

heading

column

✔ Use the **photos**, **captions**, and **diagrams** to learn more.

🔘 Selection Reading

GOOD ENOUGH TO EAT

by Lizzy Rockwell

Set Your Purpose

Find out the facts about food and why it is important.

Why Is Food Important?

When you feel hungry, sometimes your stomach **grumbles**, and your legs feel weak. Hunger sends you strong signals. It lets you know that eating is the most important thing you do each day.

The food you eat and drink keeps you alive. It builds, **protects**, and gives **energy** to your body.

Food makes you able to grow, think, breathe, move, fight germs, heal . . . and live!

Grow

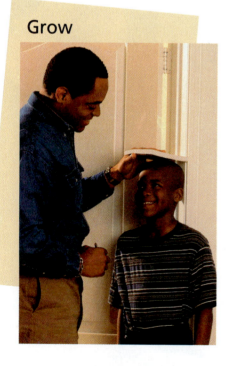

Think

---

grumbles makes noise
protects keeps you safe

Breathe and move

Fight germs

Heal

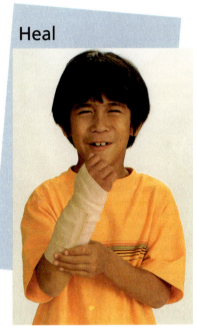

Live!

Before You Move On

1. **Details** How does your body tell you that you are hungry?

2. **Main Idea and Details** Why is food important?

What Are Nutrients?

Nutrients are the parts of food that your body uses to do its work. Every food contains at least one nutrient, but **healthy** foods have lots of them. Your body uses different nutrients in different ways.

Water is the main **ingredient in** your body. It cleans and cools you.

Carbohydrates **supply your main source of energy**. Pasta is full of carbohydrates.

Vitamins and minerals make nutrients work together. Everything your body needs to do is helped by vitamins and minerals. Vegetables have lots of vitamins and minerals.

---

ingredient in part of
supply your main source of energy give you most of your energy

Protein **supplies** energy and builds muscle, skin, and **internal organs**. Cheese has protein.

Fat supplies energy and adds flavor to foods. The butter on this bread has fat.

---

internal organs parts inside your body such as your heart, lungs, and stomach

Before You Move On

1. **Details** Name four nutrients.

2. **Classify** What nutrient is in pasta?

411

What Is Digestion?

Digestion is the way food is broken down so that nutrients can be **absorbed** into your body.

For healthy digestion you should eat plenty of fruits, vegetables, and whole grains. These foods supply **fiber**. Fiber does not get absorbed during digestion. It helps carry **bad chemicals** and **excess fats** out of your body.

---

fiber what your body needs for digestion
bad chemicals things that can harm your body
excess fats fat you don't need

▲ **This oatmeal has fiber, which helps digestion.**

The Digestive System

When you eat, the food goes through the digestive system.

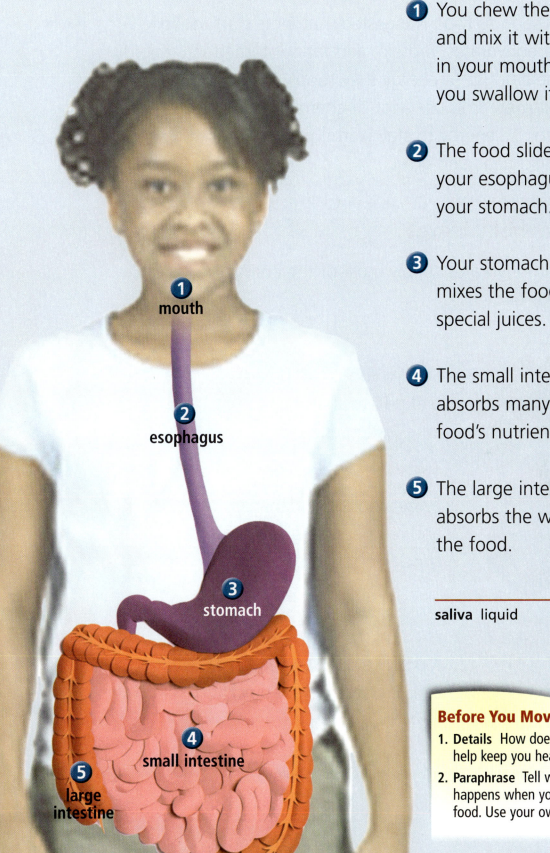

mouth

esophagus

stomach

small intestine

large intestine

1. You chew the food and mix it with **saliva** in your mouth. Then you swallow it.

2. The food slides down your esophagus to your stomach.

3. Your stomach mixes the food with special juices.

4. The small intestine absorbs many of the food's nutrients.

5. The large intestine absorbs the water in the food.

---

saliva liquid

Before You Move On

1. **Details** How does fiber help keep you healthy?
2. **Paraphrase** Tell what happens when you digest food. Use your own words.

Where Does My Energy Come From?

As soon as food is digested, nutrients start to work. Carbohydrates, protein, and fat get turned into energy. The amount of energy they supply is measured in **calories**. You use a lot of energy to run and play. You also use energy to stay warm, **pump blood**, breathe, think, heal, and grow.

Carbohydrates

Carbohydrates supply most of the energy your body uses.

Starchy foods like bread and potatoes give you long-lasting energy.

Sweet foods like bananas and red peppers give you **quick boosts of energy**.

The energy from very sweet foods like cookies and cake can be used up very quickly.

---

pump blood move blood through your body
quick boosts of energy a lot of energy soon after you eat them

Protein

Protein supplies energy. It also builds and repairs your muscles, skin, brain, blood, bones, and internal organs.

Fat

You **burn fat** for heat and energy. Fat also helps make food taste good, but it is easy to eat too much fat. Fat has more calories than the other parts of food. If you eat more calories than you need, the unused calories are turned into body fat. Eating too many fatty foods can make you heavy.

Foods with a lot of Carbohydrates	Foods with a lot of Protein	Foods with a lot of Fat
broccoli and peas	meat	ice cream
bread	beans	cake

---

burn fat use up the fat stored in your body

Before You Move On

1. **Details** Which nutrient helps the most to build muscles?

2. **Graphic Aids** How does the chart on this page explain more about nutrients?

415

What Else Helps My Body?

Water

You should drink many glasses of water every day. You don't need to worry about having too much water in your **diet**. Water is your body's main ingredient. Seventy percent of your body, including your blood, saliva, tears, and sweat, is made with water.

Why Water Is Important

- Water helps all your body systems work.

- Your body can't store water for long periods of time. You have to drink water every day.

- Even your bones have water in them. In fact, they are about one-third water.

Vitamins and Minerals

Vitamins and minerals are needed in tiny amounts to perform many important jobs in your body. They help all the nutrients in food work together.

Vitamin C helps my skin to heal.

Vitamin A helps me see well, even in the dark.

Calcium helps keep my bones and teeth strong.

Iron helps build **red blood cells**. They bring **oxygen** to my brain, heart, and muscles.

Food keeps you alive, healthy, and strong. It gives you energy and makes you grow.

Food is fun to make, and food is fun to eat!

---

red blood cells parts of my blood
oxygen air

Before You Move On

1. **Details** Name three things in your body that are made of water.
2. **Fact/Opinion** Find one fact and one opinion on page 417.

417

Think and Respond

Strategy: Main Idea and Details

What are the main ideas in "Good Enough to Eat"?
What details support each main idea? Look at this
tree diagram for pages 408–409.

Main Idea	Details
Food is important.	It keeps you alive.
	It builds, protects, and gives energy to your body.

Make a tree diagram for these main ideas:

- Pages 410–411: Food contains nutrients that help the body do its work.
- Pages 414–415: Energy comes from several sources.
- Page 417: Vitamins and minerals do important jobs.

Summarize

Work in a group of four. Each person uses a diagram to
summarize a section. Tell the main ideas and details.

Talk It Over

1 **Personal Response** Will you change the way you eat? Why or why not?

2 **Cause/Effect** What happens if you eat fruits and vegetables? What happens if you eat candies and sweets?

3 **Main Idea** Give this article a new title.

4 **Opinion** Do you think it is important to learn about nutrition and how to eat right? Why or why not?

Compare Texts

How are the graphics in "Good Enough to Eat" and "Deserts" the same? How are they different?

There are diagrams in both articles. The diagrams show how things work.

Content Connections

Talk About Exercise

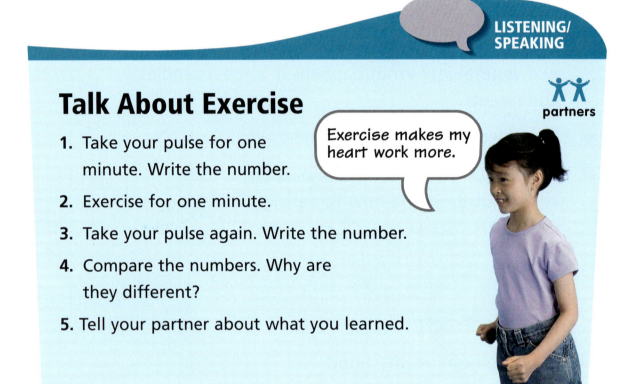

partners

1. Take your pulse for one minute. Write the number.

2. Exercise for one minute.

3. Take your pulse again. Write the number.

4. Compare the numbers. Why are they different?

5. Tell your partner about what you learned.

Exercise makes my heart work more.

Think About What You Eat

on your own

For two days, write down the food and nutrients you eat. Are you eating healthy foods? Talk about what you can do to eat healthier foods. Make a list of what you should eat.

What I Should Eat

not much chocolate
some eggs
corn
an apple

MATH

Calculate the Cost

partners

Plan a party menu. Pretend you have $50.

1. List the foods you need.

2. Find out how much each food costs. Use newspaper ads or signs at the grocery store.

3. Add the costs. Is the total more than $50? What can you do to spend less money?

Shopping List

black beans
red bell pepper
cheddar cheese
onion
garlic
pasta

WRITING

Write a Class Newsletter

large group

Internet

What questions do you have about food and nutrition? Find the answers. Then write an article to show what you learned. Combine everyone's work in a class newsletter. Share the newsletter with another class.

GRAND VIEW SCHOOL FOOD NEWS

Top 10 Vitamin C Veggies

Do you know which vegetables have the most Vitamin C? Broccoli, bell peppers, and brussels sprouts all have a lot of Vitamin C.

Adjectives That Compare

Listen and chant.

Chant

A Good Salad

Make a good salad

Out of carrots and peas.

Make it even better

With lettuce and cheese.

Add a red tomato.

Choose the very biggest one,

That will make your salad

More colorful and fun!

—Jane Zion Brauer

How Language Works

Adjectives can help you make a comparison.

-er, -est	■ Add **-er** to the adjective to compare two things.
small smaller smallest	**Example:** The yellow pepper is **smaller** than the red pepper.
	Add **-est** to compare three or more things.
	Example: The green pepper is the **smallest** of all.
more, most	■ If the adjective is a long word, use **more** or **most**.
	Examples: This pepper is **more delicious** than the green pepper.
	It is the **most colorful** of all, too.
good, better, best	■ Use special forms for **good**.
	Examples: The red pepper tastes **better** than the green one.
	This is the **best** pepper in the salad.

Practice with a Partner

Choose the correct red adjective. Then say the sentence.

more / most **1.** Grandma is the _____ wonderful cook in our family.

hotter / hottest **2.** Her red sauce is _____ than Dad's.

more / most **3.** Her rice is _____ delicious than Mom's.

bigger / biggest **4.** She makes the _____ enchiladas in town!

Put It in Writing

Think about some healthy foods you like. Compare how the foods look and taste. Use adjectives.

Mangoes are sweeter than apples.

Show What You Know

Talk About Nutrition

In this unit, you read a story and a science article about food and nutrition. Look back at the unit. Find one fact you already knew about nutrition and one fact you just learned. Share your facts with a partner.

Make a Mind Map

Work with a partner. Make a chart to show what you learned about nutrition.

Food and Your Body		
Food	Nutrient	What It Does for My Body
pasta	carbohydrates	gives me energy

Think and Write

What can you do to become healthier? Make a list. Add this writing to your portfolio. Include work from this unit that shows what you learned about nutrition.

Read and Learn More

Leveled Books

**Lunch at the
Joy House Cafe**
by Susan Blackaby

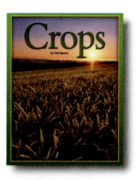

Crops
by Fred Ignacio

Theme Library

**I Have a Weird
Brother Who
Digested a Fly**
by Joan Holub

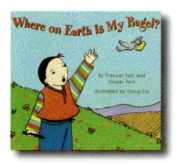

**Where on Earth Is
My Bagel?**
by Frances Park and
Ginger Park

Internet

Go to: www.hbavenues.com

Fruits and Veggies

Nutrition Game

More Nutrition Games

Family Gifts

Create a Special Gift

What gift have you received from an older family member? What special gift would you pass on to someone in your family?

1. Make a box.
2. Draw a picture of the gift and put it in the box. Add a tag.
3. Tell about your gift.

Family Traditions

Tell Stories

▲ Parents read with their daughter.

▲ Dancers tell a Polynesian legend.

▲ A family shares stories around a campfire.

Eat Special Meals

▲ A family celebrates the end of Ramadan with a special meal.

▲ Everyone helps make Thanksgiving dinner.

▲ A family celebrates Chinese New Year.

Celebrate Together

▲ A grandfather helps his grandson light Hanukkah candles.

▲ Everyone helps to make decorations for the Day of the Dead.

▲ Kwanzaa is a special time for this family.

Learn from Each Other

▲ A boy learns from his mother.

▲ A Navajo girl learns to weave from her grandmother.

▲ A father teaches his daughter to play baseball.

A Special Letter

Act out the conversation.

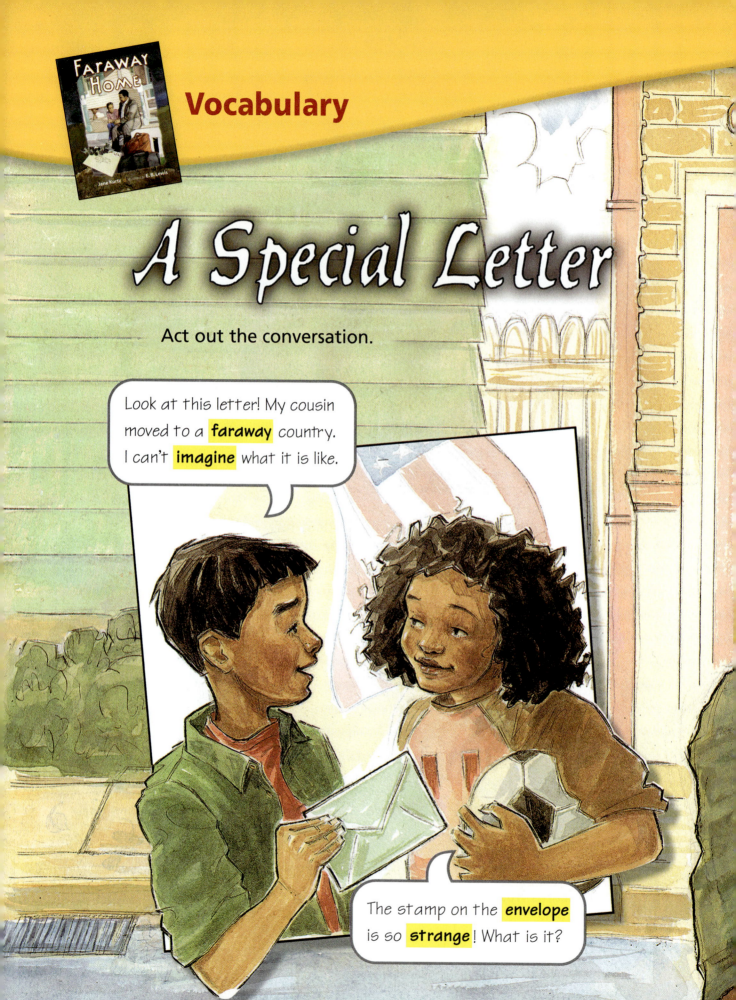

Look at this letter! My cousin moved to a **faraway** country. I can't **imagine** what it is like.

The stamp on the **envelope** is so **strange**! What is it?

That is a flamingo. My cousin says they are very **proud** of these animals in his country.

I'd like to hear more! I wish I didn't I have to **leave** for soccer practice.

Key Words

faraway

imagine

envelope

strange

proud

leave

Faraway Home

by **Jane Kurtz**   illustrated by **E. B. Lewis**

ADIKAS TERAFA
6146 S. HERBY AVE.
PORTLAND OR 97211
USA

Read a Story

Genre

This story tells about events that could really happen. It is <mark>realistic fiction</mark>. In this story, a girl worries because her father must go on a long trip.

Characters

Desta

Desta's father

Setting

This story happens in Desta's house in the United States. Her father has to go to Ethiopia for a while.

U.S.

Ethiopia

Selection Reading

1

Desta's grandmother is sick. How will Desta's life change?

When Desta dances into her house after school, the first thing she sees is the green **envelope**. She traces the bright stamp with her finger.

"Your grandmother back home in Ethiopia is ill," her mother explains. "Your father needs to go home to be with her."

"Daddy is going to **leave** us?" Desta runs to her father's favorite chair and **curls up** in it.

---

curls up sits with her legs folded under her

When evening comes, **soft as a curtain closing**,
Desta's father takes her in his arms. He tells her again
that *desta* means "joy," and sings a **haunting** song full
of words she doesn't know.

"Ethiopia is so far away," Desta says. "I don't want
you to go."

---

soft as a curtain closing slowly and gently
haunting sad

Before You Move On

1. **Cause/Effect** Why does the letter make Desta sad?

2. **Inference** Why does Desta's father remind her that her name means "joy"?

Find out what Desta learns about Ethiopia from her father.

"**F**or me, Ethiopia is never far away," her father says.

"Close your eyes and try to see green-gray mountains. Think about a thick cloud of fog **crawling** up the valley and the lonely sound of cowbells in the hills."

Desta closes her eyes and hears the **wind chime** hanging from the front porch. "Do cowbells sound like that?" she thinks.

---

crawling moving slowly
wind chime small bells that ring in the wind

"When I was your age," Desta's father says, "I carried **grain** on my head to the mill by the waterfall, where the grain was **ground** into flour. Then my mother made *injera* and cooked it over the fire that **lived in a scooped-out place** in the middle of the floor."

Desta shakes her head. In her home, the fire stays in a fireplace. Her own mother cooks *injera* on the stove.

---

grain wheat
ground crushed
injera a thin bread (from Ethiopia)
lived in a scooped-out place was in a little hole

437

"My friend Christopher says Africa is hot," Desta tells her father.

He **clicks** his tongue. "Not where I lived. Sometimes at night the **wind whooshed cold as old bones** through the silver blue leaves of the eucalyptus trees outside my home. I slept on the floor wrapped in my *gabi* to keep warm."

Desta tries to imagine sleeping on the floor and listening to silver blue eucalyptus. The tree <u>she</u> hears at night drops white blossoms on her bedroom windowsill, blossoms that look like snow.

---

clicks makes a noise with
wind whooshed cold as old bones cold wind blew
gabi thick cotton blanket or covering (from Ethiopia)

"In Ethiopia," her father says in a **faraway** voice, "hippos yawn from muddy pools and crocodiles **arch** their backs above the river water. **Shepherds pipe songs of longing** in the hills, and thousands of **flamingos flap in a pink cloud** over the Great Rift Valley lakes. I wish you could see the pink cloud."

arch raise

Shepherds pipe songs of longing People play sad songs as they watch the sheep

flamingos flap in a pink cloud pink birds fly close together

"Did you walk to school like I do?" Desta asks.

"Yes," her father says. "And I carried a stick of purple sugarcane over my shoulder. Sometimes I couldn't wait for lunch. I chewed out the sweet juices as I walked to school with mud squeezing up between my toes."

Desta stares at her father. "Why did you take your shoes off?"

He laughs. "I didn't wear shoes to school."

"You didn't wear shoes?" Desta thinks of the shoes in her closet. She has the black pair, the wonderful red pair, and the new pair that she can hardly wait to wear. "No shoes," she says. "That's **strange**."

Before You Move On

1. **Comparison** How is Desta's childhood different from her father's childhood in Ethiopia?

2. **Opinion** Does Ethiopia seem interesting? Why?

441

3

Find out why Desta worries about her father's trip.

Desta's father gives her a mule ride to bed. He switches on her night-light and takes her hand in his. "Desta," he says, "**my stomach is always hungry** to go home. Now my *emayay* is very sick. It is time for me to go home and be with her for a while."

Desta thinks of hippos and crocodiles and a cold whooshing wind. "Daddy," she says, "would you like to take my night-light with you?"

"Thank you," her father says, "but my mother's home has no **electricity**."

---

my stomach is always hungry I always want
emayay mama (in Amharic, an Ethiopian language)
electricity power for lights

"When I was a boy, sometimes **the darkness pressed against me**, and I heard the hyenas' strange coughing cry close by. But my *emayay* sang to me. She showed me that sunsets were bright borders on the cloth of the evening sky. The moon and stars burned holes in the cloth to light the night."

---

the darkness pressed against me I felt scared in the dark

Desta looks out the window at the stars beyond the snow blossom tree. She **shivers to think** of the hyenas' cry. "Don't leave us to go there," she says. "Your home is too wild."

A sad look flies over her father's face, and before Desta goes to sleep, she hears him singing the haunting song with words she doesn't understand.

---

shivers to think gets scared when she thinks

Before You Move On

1. **Inference** Why does Desta want to give her night-light to her father?

2. **Details** Why did Desta's father get scared sometimes at night?

4

Will Desta
change her
mind about her
father's trip?

The next morning Desta walks to school, **scuffing** the toes of her shoes on the sidewalk. The wind chime rings in rhymes all the way down her block. Why does her father have to remember things like cowbells and silver blue eucalyptus? What if he goes away and never comes back?

---

scuffing dragging

Desta dreams all morning by the window. At lunchtime she asks Christopher, "Did you ever hear of anyone not wearing shoes to school?"

"No," he says. "That would be **weird**."

Desta frowns. When Christopher leaves, she opens her locket and looks at the face of the grandmother she has never met but whose picture she wears close to her heart. Her grandmother's eyes always look back at her, <mark>proud</mark> and strong. But is there also **sadness glimmering in those eyes**?

---

weird strange
sadness glimmering in those eyes a sad
look in her eyes

▲ **locket**

In the afternoon, Desta **looks up** flamingos in the teacher's big book. As she studies their upside-down smiles, she thinks she almost hears the sound of a haunting **lullaby** somewhere at the edge of the classroom. After school she walks home barefoot, swinging her shoes, feeling the sun under her feet where it has soaked into the ground.

---

looks up reads about
lullaby song

When evening comes, soft as a curtain closing, Desta climbs into her father's lap. "I think you miss your home a lot," she says.

"Yes, I do," her father says.

Desta **sighs**. "And your *emayay* misses you a lot."

"Yes," he says. "The same way I will miss you while I am gone."

"Will you tell me about your home every night until you leave?" Desta asks.

Her father holds her close. "Oh yes," he says. "And when I come back—and I <u>will</u> come back—I will have new stories to tell."

"Know what?" Desta says. "Shoes aren't so great."

Desta **catches** her father's smile and then closes her eyes. He will come back. Until he does, she can **hold his stories in her heart**.

---

sighs makes a sad noise

catches sees

hold his stories in her heart think about his stories and feel like he is there with her

Before You Move On

1. **Inference** Why does Desta walk home barefoot?

2. **Cause/Effect** Why does Desta change her mind about her father's trip?

451

Meet the Illustrator

E. B. Lewis

Earl Bradley Lewis began to paint in the third grade. His two uncles were artists. Their work inspired him to become an artist, too. Now Mr. Lewis illustrates children's books. Many of his books, like *Faraway Home*, show African American families.

Mr. Lewis visits schools as often as he can. He tells stories and shows students how he makes his artwork. He always signs books for kids. In each book, he adds a message like "Follow your passion." That means to do the things you really care about.

Where My Grandmother Lived

Where my grandmother lived
there was always sweet potato pie
and thirds on green beans and
songs and words of how we'd
survived it all.
Blackness.
And the wind
a soft lull
in the pecan tree
whispered
Ethiopia, Ethiopia, Ethiopia
E-th-io-piaaaaa!

—*Doughtry Long*

Before You Move On

Personal Response Where does your grandmother live? What is it like there?

Think and Respond

Strategy: Cause and Effect

In some stories, one event makes another event happen.
In these stories, look for:

✔ the cause, or the reason something happens
✔ the effect, or what happens.

Make a chart. Show the causes and effects in "Faraway Home."

Faraway Home

Pages	Cause	Effects
434–435	Desta's grandmother gets sick.	Desta's father must go to Ethiopia. Desta is upset, so he tries to comfort her.
436–441	Desta's father tells about his childhood.	
442–445	Desta hears about the darkness and how the wild animals come out at night in Ethiopia.	Desta tries to give her father her night-light to keep him safe while he is in Ethiopia.
446–451	Desta worries.	

Retell the Story

Use your chart to retell the story. Talk about how Desta feels.

Talk It Over

1. **Personal Response** How would you feel if someone in your family had to go far away on a long trip?

2. **Comparison** Life for Desta's father is different in the United States than his life in Ethiopia. How? How is it the same?

3. **Inference** Desta's father says, "Ethiopia is never far away." What does he mean?

4. **Author's Purpose** Why do you think Jane Kurtz wrote this story?

Compare Ideas

What does the poet remember about Ethiopia? What does Desta's father remember about it?

Both people remember the wind in Ethiopia.

Content Connections

Act Out a Scene

partners

What do you think Desta's father will do while he is in Ethiopia? With your partner, role-play a new scene for the story. Present your scene to the class.

Hi, emayay. Can I do something for you?

Compare Characters

small group

Compare the grandmother in "A Picnic in October" with the father in "Faraway Home." Think about where they come from and how they feel.

	Where from	Actions	Feelings
Grandma	Italy	celebrates the Statue of Liberty's birthday every year	loves her new country
Father	Ethiopia	tells stories about Ethiopia	likes his new country, but misses his old country

456

Make an Ethiopian Animal Reserve

Internet

large group

Find out about one animal that lives in Ethiopia. Use the facts you find to make a chart about the animal. Add your chart and a picture of the animal to a class display. Tell your class about the animal.

Flamingos

color	red or pink
height	up to 61 inches
life span	20-60 years

WRITING

Write a Book Review

on your own

Tell a friend or someone in your family about "Faraway Home." Describe the characters and the plot. In your review of the story, tell why your friend should or should not read it. Then e-mail your review.

FROM:
TO: tiarosa@newyorknet.com

subject: a great story

I read a great story about Ethiopia. It's called "Faraway Home," and it was written by Jane Kurtz. Now I want to go to there and see the flamingos.

Make Predictions

When you guess what will happen next in a story, you <mark>make a prediction</mark>. To make predictions:

- ✔ Read carefully and look for story clues.
- ✔ Think about what you already know.
- ✔ Make a guess about what will happen next.
- ✔ Then read to find out if your prediction is right.

Try the strategy.

from FARAWAY HOME

When Desta dances into her house after school, the first thing she sees is the green envelope. She traces the bright stamp with her finger.

"Your grandmother back home in Ethiopia is ill," her mother explains. "Your father needs to go home to be with her."

"Daddy is going to leave us?" Desta runs to her father's favorite chair and curls up in it.

> Desta asks if her dad is leaving them and then sits in his favorite chair. I feel sad when my dad goes on a trip. I predict that Desta will miss her father.

Practice

Take this test and **make predictions** about "Faraway Home."

Read each item. Choose the best answer.

1 **Which of the following is <u>not</u> a good prediction about Desta?**

- ⬭ She will go to Ethiopia some day.
- ⬭ She will never wear her locket again.
- ⬭ She will want to learn more about Ethiopia.
- ⬭ She will be happy when her father returns from his trip.

> ✅ **Test Strategy**
>
> Check your answers if you have time. Reread the questions and the answers you marked.

2 **Look at this diagram of story clues.**

| Detail:
Desta's father lives with his family in the United States. | + | Detail:
Desta's father will miss her when he is in Ethiopia. | = | Prediction: |

- ⬭ Desta's father will stay in Ethiopia.
- ⬭ Desta's family will move to Ethiopia.
- ⬭ Desta's father will come back from Ethiopia.
- ⬭ Desta's grandmother will move to the United States.

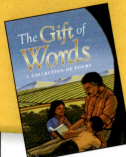

Song

My Grandparents

My grandparents came to this country.

They ==came from== way over the sea.

When we get ==together== they tell us

The ==story== of our ==family==.

Look back, way back,

Tell us what life was like long ago.

Think back, way back,

So each generation will know.

—Joyce McGreevy

Tune: "My Bonnie Lies Over the Ocean"

461

Read Poetry

Poems use colorful language to tell about ideas. Poems can tell stories or explain feelings.

✔ **Stanzas** divide the poem into parts.

stanza

My Grandma's Stories

Mita's **stories**
filled her **shack**
with stars

Mita's stories
put smiles
on our faces

✔ Say the poems out loud. Listen for the beat, or **rhythm**, the words make. Some poems have words that **rhyme**, too.

🔘 Selection Reading

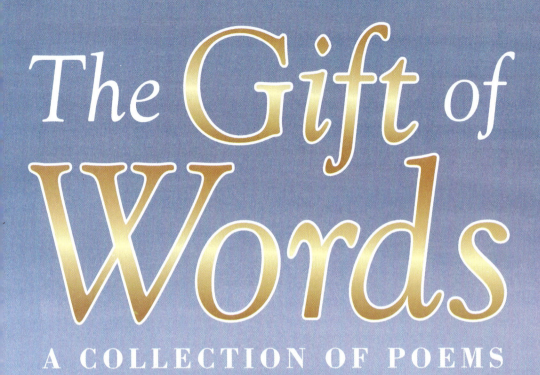

The Gift of Words

A COLLECTION OF POEMS

Set Your Purpose

Learn about some special family gifts. Have you received gifts like them?

My Grandma's Stories

Mita's **stories**
filled her **shack**
with stars

Mita's stories
put smiles
on our faces

Mita's stories
are old
like the mountains

Mita's stories
are like the songs
of the **crickets**

If I close my eyes
I hear them
in the wind

—*Jorge Argueta*

Mita's stories My grandmother's stories
shack small house
crickets insects that make noise at night

464

Meet the Poet

Jorge Argueta calls his grandmother "Mita," which is from the Spanish words "mi abuelita." When Mr. Argueta moved to the United States from El Salvador, his grandma stayed behind.

Before You Move On

1. **Inference** Why are Mita's stories like gifts?
2. **Personal Experience** Tell your partner a story from your family.

465

FAMILY GIFTS

Grandpa came from Russia,
He brought a coin with him,
A coin his dad had given,
He sewed it in **his hem**.

He always rubbed it in his hand,
Until the picture **blurred**,
One day he **slipped it in my palm**
And didn't say a word.

—Judith Steinbergh

his hem the folded fabric at the
bottom of his clothing
blurred was hard to see
slipped it in my palm put it in my hand

Meet the Poet

Judith Steinbergh's father gave her a special gift. She says, "My father gave me the language to see the world differently." Ms. Steinbergh has used that gift to write and teach poetry to school children.

Before You Move On

1. **Inference** Why is the coin a special gift?
2. **Rhyme** Which words in this poem rhyme? Say them.

My name

My name came from my
   great-great-great
   grandfather.
He was an Indian from the
   Choctaw tribe.
His name was Dark Ant.
When he went to get a job
   out in a city
he changed it to Emmett.
And his whole name was
   Emmett Perez Tenorio.
And my name means: Ant;
   Strong; Carry twice its size.

—*Emmett Tenorio Meléndez*

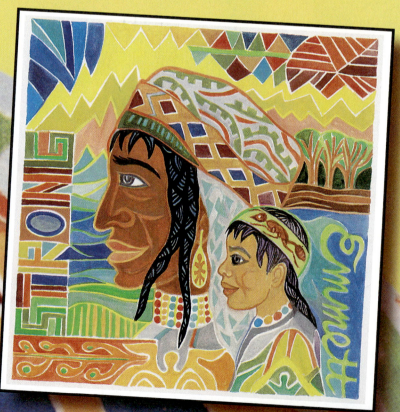

Another Kid

I was just another kid
in T-shirt and blue jeans
until Grandmother gave me
new **beaded moccasins**.

—*Virginia Driving Hawk Sneve*

---

beaded moccasins soft shoes
decorated with beads

Meet the Poets

Emmett Tenorio Meléndez
wrote this poem in school.
His teacher collected her
favorite poems and published
them in a book called
Salting the Ocean.

AWARD WINNER

**Virginia Driving Hawk
Sneve** could not find
books to teach her
children about being
Native American. So,
she began to write
about her Native
heritage. Her writing
became her gift to her
family and to the world.

Before You Move On

1. **Cause/Effect** How do the moccasins change the child in Ms. Sneve's poem?

2. **Personal Experience** What does your name mean to you? Why?

In Our One Family

In our one **family**, around
               this
        round
         table
of our nights and days:
          we are **together**
          in old ways,
          we are together
          in new ways.
Pancakes and chicken. Pork chops and cream:
      we
        are new people
          eating our way
to a new time
        of
      love

          We are trying for the
              dream.
          —*Arnold Adoff*

Meet the Poet

Arnold Adoff often writes about his family. Mr. Adoff's ancestors came from Poland. His wife, author Virginia Hamilton, was African American. They combined old traditions from their own families to create new traditions for their children.

Before You Move On

1. **Inference** What is the poet's message?
2. **Personal Experience** How does your family mix old and new traditions?

471

December's Song

My daddy's washed his **bricklayer hands**
Red and muddy with **mortar**

Now he smells like houses
In their early stages

Like the fireplace
He's built and **stoked** with wood
As it flashes bright
Enough to warm my chilly bones

---

bricklayer hands hands that he uses to put bricks in place
mortar a mixture that holds bricks together
In their early stages That he is building
stoked filled

His **chapped** hands are brave
With work
Rough with knowing
How to keep a family from freezing
How to keep a young mind growing

He is a gift all by himself
His hands ungloved
His heat, his love

It's December
And of all the gifts December brings
I'll always remember
That people are more important than things

—*Joyce Carol Thomas*

chapped cracked, rough

Meet the Poet

Joyce Carol Thomas has loved words for as long as she can remember. She looks closely at people to find their beauty, their stories, and their love of life. She then writes about them and passes this gift on to others.

Before You Move On

1. **Character** What is the father like?

2. **Figurative Language** What does the poet mean when she says, "He is a gift all by himself"?

475

Think and Respond

Strategy: Relate to Personal Experience

The poets talk about different kinds of family gifts. List the gifts in a chart. What gifts can you add?

Gifts in the Poems	Gifts I Know About
stories Grandma told	
Grandpa's coin	
Grandpa's name	
beaded moccasins	
traditional family meals	
Dad's love	

Draw Conclusions

Look at your chart. Think about the different kinds of gifts families give. Why do you think families give gifts to each other?

Talk It Over

1 **Personal Response** Which is your favorite poem? Explain.

2 **Comparison** Compare the gifts in "My Grandma's Stories" on page 464 and "Family Gifts" on page 466.

3 **Opinion** Do you think poetry is a good way to express feelings? Why or why not?

4 **Judgments** Which family gift do you think is most valuable? Why?

Compare Topics

What gifts does Desta receive from her family? How do these gifts compare to the ones in the poems?

Content Connections

LISTENING/ SPEAKING

Teach a Greeting

on your own

Mr. Argueta calls his grandmother Mita. What do you call your relatives? Teach the class what you say to greet your family members.

Strasvitya, Mama!

ART

Illustrate Your Name

On your own

What does your name mean to you? Why were you named the way you were? Make a drawing of your name. Use your drawing to tell the class why your name is special.

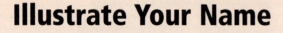

small group

Tell About Traditions

Internet

Learn about a tradition from a culture other than your own. It could be a craft, a food, a song, or a story. Show your class how to make it or tell it.

origami

partners

Write a Poem

Write a poem to tell about a family member, a family's traditions, or your experiences. Read your new poem to your partner.

If I close my eyes
I see
Our one family.
And all around me
There are smiles
As warm
As a desert night.

Pronouns

Listen and sing.

Song

See Us Shine

We are all children of the world.
We are all children of the world.
We are all children of the world.
We are together. See us shine!

She is from China. See her shine.
He is from Brazil. See him shine.
They are from Russia. See them shine.
We are together. See us shine!

—*Jane Zion Brauer*

Tune: "He's Got the Whole World in His Hands"

How Language Works

A **pronoun** can take the place of a noun.

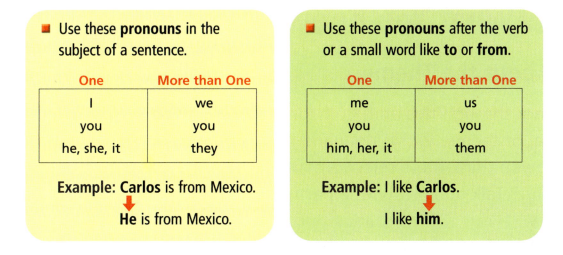

■ Use these **pronouns** in the subject of a sentence.

One	More than One
I	we
you	you
he, she, it	they

Example: **Carlos** is from Mexico.

He is from Mexico.

■ Use these **pronouns** after the verb or a small word like **to** or **from**.

One	More than One
me	us
you	you
him, her, it	them

Example: I like **Carlos**.

I like **him**.

Practice with a Partner

Choose the correct red pronoun. Then say the sentence.

I / Me   1. _____ want to visit my grandparents.

They / Them 2. _____ live in El Salvador.

they / them 3. I call _____ on the phone.

us / you   4. "When can I visit _____?" I ask.

we / us   5. "Come visit _____ soon !" they say.

Put It in Writing

Write about a visit you made to someone. When you edit your work, make sure the pronouns are correct.

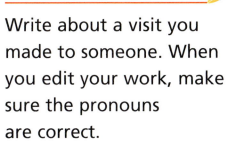

We drove in our car to Aunt Lupe's house. She made chicken mole for us.

Show What You Know

Talk About the Theme

Look back through this unit. Compare the big idea, or theme, in the story and poems. Why do you think these selections are in the same unit? Talk about it with a partner.

Make a Mind Map

Make a mind map to show why family gifts are important. First list gifts from the story and poems. Then list gifts from your own family.

Family Gift	Why the Gift Is Important
father's stories	changed Desta's mind about her father's trip
locket	reminded Desta of her grandmother

Think and Write

Think about what gifts you have given to your family. Make a list. Add this writing to your portfolio. Include work that shows what you learned about family gifts.

Read and Learn More

Leveled Books

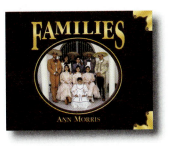

Families
by Ann Morris

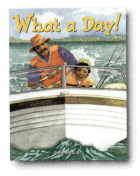

What a Day!
by Anne Miranda

Theme Library

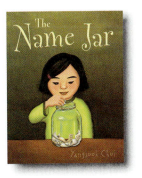

The Name Jar
by Yangsook Choi

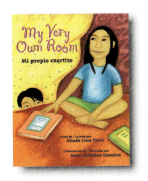

My Very Own Room
by Amada Irma Perez

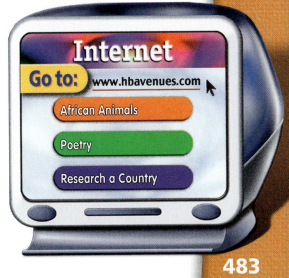

Internet

Go to: www.hbavenues.com

African Animals

Poetry

Research a Country

Picture Dictionary

The definitions are for the words as they are introduced in the selections in this book.

Pronunciation Key

Say the sample word out loud to hear how to say, or pronounce, the symbol.

Symbols for Consonant Sounds

b	box	p	pan	
ch	chick	r	ring	
d	dog	s	bus	
f	fish	sh	fish	
g	girl	t	hat	
h	hat	th	Earth	
j	jar	th	father	
k	cake	v	vase	
ks	box	w	window	
kw	queen	wh	whale	
l	bell	y	yarn	
m	mouse	z	zipper	
n	pan	zh	treasure	
ng	ring			

Symbols for Short Vowel Sounds

a	hat
e	bell
i	chick
o	box
u	bus

Symbols for Long Vowel Sounds

ā	cake
ē	key
ī	bike
ō	goat
ū	fruit
yū	mule

Symbols for R-controlled Sounds

ar	barn
air	chair
or	corn
ur	girl
īr	fire

Symbols for Variant Vowel Sounds

ah	father
aw	ball
oi	boy
ow	mouse
oo	book

Miscellaneous Symbols

shun	fraction	$\frac{1}{2}$
chun	question	**?**
zhun	division	$2\overline{)100}^{\,50}$

Parts of an Entry

The **entry** shows how the word is spelled.

The **pronunciation** shows you how to say the word and how to break it into syllables.

The **picture** helps you understand more about the meaning of the word.

island

(ī-lund) *noun*

An **island** is a piece of land that has water all around it.

boat

island

*You have to take a boat to get to and from the **island**.*

part of speech

The **definition** gives the meaning of the word.

The **sample** sentence uses the word in a way that shows its meaning.

A

absorb
(ab-**zorb**) *verb*

Absorb means to take in something and hold it.

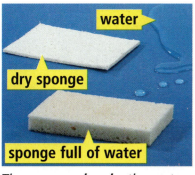
water
dry sponge
sponge full of water

*The sponge **absorbs** the water.*

adapt
(a-**dapt**) *verb*

When you **adapt**, you change to fit a new situation.

*You **adapt** to the cold by wearing a coat.*

astronaut
(**as**-tru-nawt) *noun*

An **astronaut** is a person who travels to outer space in a spacecraft.

*This **astronaut** works in space.*

B

beautiful
(**byū**-ti-ful) *adjective*

Something that is very pretty is **beautiful.**

*Look at the **beautiful** flowers!*

branch
(branch) *noun*

A **branch** is a part of a tree that grows out from the trunk.

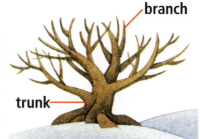
branch
trunk

*The **branches** of this tree do not have leaves in the winter.*

breeze
(brēz) *noun*

A **breeze** is a light, gentle wind.

*The **breeze** lifts the kite into the air.*

C

calorie
(**kal**-u-rē) *noun*

Food gives you energy. A **calorie** is a measurement of how much energy is in a food.

one apple, 81 calories

three pancakes, 270 calories

one ounce of peanuts, 165 calories

*A child should eat about 2000 **calories** a day.*

came from
(kām frum) *verb*

The place that you **came from** is the place where you were born.

before
now

*I **came from** Illinois, but now I live in Florida.*
<u>In the present:</u> *I **come from** Illinois.*

485

canyon
(**kan**-yun) *noun*

A **canyon** is a deep, narrow piece of land with very steep sides.

*This **canyon** has steep, red rock walls.*

change
(chānj) *verb*

When something **changes**, it becomes different.

spring   summer

fall   winter

*How does the tree **change** in each season?*

city council
(sit-ē **kown**-sul) *noun*

A **city council** is a group of people elected to run a city or town.

council members

*The **city council** votes on a new law.*

cloud
(klowd) *noun*

A **cloud** is a mass of tiny drops of water floating in the air.

cloud

community
(ku-**myū**-nu-tē) *noun*

A **community** is a group of people who live in the same place.

*These neighbors like their **community**.*

connect
(ku-**nekt**) *verb*

When you **connect** with other people, you learn about them and feel closer to them.

*This teacher **connects** with her students when she talks to them.*

convince
(kun-**vins**) *verb*

Convince means to make a person think like you think or do what you want to do.

not convinced

SALE 8⁹⁸

convinced

SALE 8⁹⁸

*Jorge **convinced** his mom to buy the CD.*

crater
(krā-tur) *noun*

When something hits the Moon, it makes a **crater**. A crater is shaped like a bowl.

*A rock from space made this huge **crater** in the Moon.*

D

dangerous
(**dān**-jur-us) *adjective*

Something that is **dangerous** can hurt you.

*Crossing this street can be very **dangerous**.*

decision
(di-**sizh**-un) *noun*

When you make a **decision**, you make up your mind about something.

*She makes a **decision** about which shirt to wear.*

desert floor
(**dez**-urt flor) *noun*

The **desert floor** is the flat ground in a desert.

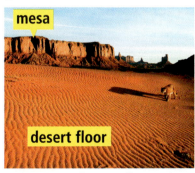

mesa

desert floor

*A mountain lion walks across the **desert floor**.*

diet
(**dī**-it) *noun*

A **diet** is what a person eats and drinks.

milk   chicken   vegetables   fruit   bread

*These foods are part of a healthy **diet**.*

digestion
(dī-**jes**-chun) *noun*

Digestion is the process your body uses to break down food into smaller pieces. This helps your body use the food.

Digestive System

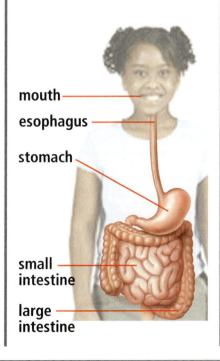

mouth
esophagus
stomach
small intestine
large intestine

disappear
(dis-u-**pēr**) *verb*

When something **disappears**, it goes away.

*The snowman **disappears** when the sun shines on it.*

dream
(drēm) *noun*

A **dream** is something you think about and hope to do someday.

*Fox and Mole tell each other about their **dreams**.*

dune
(dūn) *noun*

A **dune** is a hill made of sand.

*The wind blew the sand and made this **dune**.*

E

energy
(**en**-ur-jē) *noun*

Energy is the power to do work.

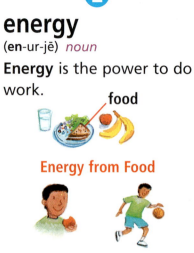

Energy from Food

When you eat food, you get **energy** *to work and play.*

envelope
(**en**-vu-lōp) *noun*

When you want to mail a letter or a card, you put it in an **envelope**. It is made of paper.

The girl puts the card in an **envelope**.

experience
(eks-**pēr**-ē-uns) *noun*

Things that you have done and seen in your life are your **experiences**.

She tells about her **experiences** *when she was younger.*

F

fall
(fawl) *verb*

Something **falls** when it drops down from a higher place.

In the past:
It **fell**.
It **has fallen**.

The leaves **fall** *from the tree when the wind blows.*

family
(**fam**-u-lē) *noun*

A **family** is a group of people who are related to one another.

There are five people in this **family**.

faraway
(far-u-**wā**) *adjective*

A **faraway** place is a place that is not close to you.

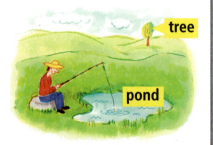

The **faraway** *tree cannot give shade to the fisherman.*

ferry
(**fair**-ē) *noun*

A **ferry** is a kind of boat. It takes people and cars across the water from one place to another.

The **ferry** *sails from the city to the island.*

flower
(**flow**-ur) *noun*

A **flower** is the part of a plant that makes seeds. Flowers often have petals with bright colors.

The **flower** *of this plant looks like the sun.*

forget
(fur-**get**) *verb*

You **forget** something when you don't remember it.

In the past:
He **forgot**.
He **has forgotten**.

Marcel often **forgets** *his lunch.*

found

(fownd) *verb*

If you **found** something, you looked for it and got it back.

In the present:
*He **finds** his shoe.*

*He **found** his shoe under the bed.*

frost

(frawst) *noun*

Frost is a very thin layer of frozen water.

frost

*You see **frost** on the window when the weather is very cold.*

G

garden

(**gar**-dun) *noun*

A **garden** is a piece of land where you grow flowers or vegetables.

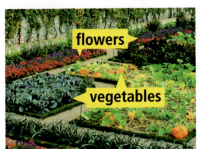

flowers

vegetables

*We planted flowers and vegetables in our **garden**.*

government

(**guv**-urn-munt) *noun*

The **government** is the group of people who make laws for a country, a state, or a city.

council member

mayor

*The mayor and council are part of the city **government**.*

greedy

(**grē**-dē) *adjective*

Greedy people want more of something. They do not share what they have.

*The **greedy** people kept summer for themselves.*

gully

(**gul**-ē) *noun*

A **gully** is a narrow ditch made by moving water.

gully

*A stream made this **gully** in the ground.*

H

healthy

(**hel**-thē) *adjective*

When you eat **healthy** food, your body grows strong and you feel well.

***Healthy** foods are good for your body.*

helpful

(**help**-ful) *adjective*

You are **helpful** when you do something useful for someone.

*Tony is **helpful**.*

hill

(hil) *noun*

A **hill** is higher than the land around it.

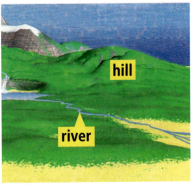

hill

river

*The river goes past the **hills**.*

489

homesick

(hōm-sik) *adjective*

When you feel **homesick**, you are sad because you are away from your home or family.

*After she moved to Texas, she was **homesick** for her family in Korea.*

I

idea

(ī-**dē**-u) *noun*

An **idea** is something a person thinks or imagines.

*He had a good **idea** about a way to blow out his birthday candles.*

---

imagine

(i-**maj**-in) *verb*

When you **imagine** something, you make a picture of it in your mind.

*Tim **imagines** what he will do on his camping trip.*

immigrant

(**im**-u-grunt) *noun*

An **immigrant** is a person who leaves one country and goes to another country to live.

*These **immigrants** were born in Russia. They came to the United States to make a new life.*

---

important

(im-**port**-unt) *adjective*

Something is **important** when it has great meaning or value.

*Alma gives Mom an **important** letter from school.*

impossible

(im-**pos**-u-bul) *adjective*

If something is **impossible**, it cannot happen.

*It is **impossible** for the boy to flap his arms and fly.*

---

island

(ī-lund) *noun*

An **island** is a piece of land that has water all around it.

boat island

*You have to take a boat to get to and from the **island**.*

J

journey

(**jur**-nē) *noun*

A **journey** is a trip.

*These families took the long **journey** from their homelands to the United States.*

L

leave

(lēv) *verb*

When you **leave**, you go away from a place.

*She **leaves** school and goes home at 3 o'clock.*

life cycle

(līf sī-kul) *noun*

A **life cycle** is a set of changes in a plant or an animal. These changes always happen in the same order.

Life Cycle of a Pea Plant

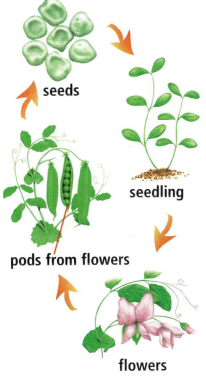

seeds

seedling

pods from flowers

flowers

lost

(lawst) *adjective*

When something is **lost**, you do not have it or know where it is.

a necklace   no necklace

*She can't find her **lost** necklace.*

M

map

(map) *noun*

A **map** is a drawing of Earth's surface. Some maps show continents, countries, and landforms. Other maps show cities, roads, climate, and products.

World Map

mayor

(mā-ur) *noun*

A **mayor** is the leader of a city or town government.

*The **mayor** makes important decisions.*

meal

(mēl) *noun*

A **meal** is food that you eat at a certain time. Breakfast, lunch, and dinner are meals.

*What does she eat at this **meal**?*

melt

(melt) *verb*

When something **melts**, heat turns it from a solid into a liquid.

*Ice cream **melts** quickly on a hot day.*

memory
(**mem**-u-rē) *noun*

A **memory** is something that you think about now but that happened in the past.

a memory

*I learned to ride a bike when I was six. It is a good **memory**.*

menu
(**men**-yū) *noun*

A **menu** is a list of the food you can order in a restaurant.

price

food

*What do you want to order from the **menu**?*

meteorite
(mē-tē-u-**rīt**) *noun*

A **meteorite** is a rock that flies through space and hits the land.

*This **meteorite** hits the Moon.*

mineral
(**min**-ur-ul) *noun*

A **mineral** is something in nature, like salt, that is not a plant or an animal.

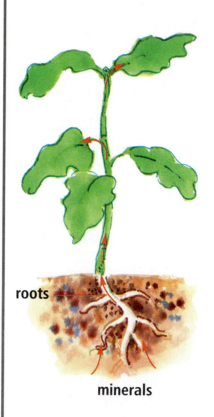

roots

minerals

*The roots get water and **minerals** from the soil.*

mountain
(**mown**-tun) *noun*

A **mountain** is a very high place. It is higher than a hill.

*This **mountain** is covered with snow.*

nature
(**nā**-chur) *noun*

Nature is everything in the world that is not made by people.

*Many people enjoy the beauty of **nature**.*

neighborhood
(nā-bur-**hood**) *noun*

A **neighborhood** is an area where people live and work.

house

store

street

*This **neighborhood** is in a city.*

492

nutrient

(**nū**-trē-unt) *noun*

A **nutrient** is a part of food that living things need to grow and stay healthy.

*These foods are full of **nutrients**, like protein, vitamins, and minerals.*

---

petition

(pu-**tish**-un) *noun*

A **petition** is a letter that asks for something. It is signed by many people.

Town of Concord
Petition for New School
1. Susan Clark
2.
3.
4. Anna Jones

*This **petition** asks the mayor for a new school.*

---

plan

(plan) *noun*

When you have a **plan**, you have an idea for getting something done.

My Plan
1. Make bed.
2. Put away clothes.
3. Throw away junk.
4. Clean desk.
5. Relax!

*This is a **plan** for cleaning a bedroom.*

possible

(**pos**-u-bul) *adjective*

Something is **possible** when it can or might happen.

*It is **possible** that it will rain today.*

---

prepare

(pri-**pair**) *verb*

When you **prepare** something, you get it ready to use.

*Mom, Ricky, and Ana **prepare** a fresh salad.*

---

prey

(prā) *noun*

An animal is **prey** if another animal hunts it for food.

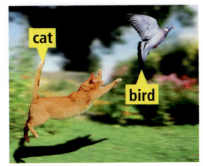

*The bird is the **prey** of the cat.*

process

(**pro**-ses) *noun*

A **process** is a set of steps that happen in a certain order.

Making Candles

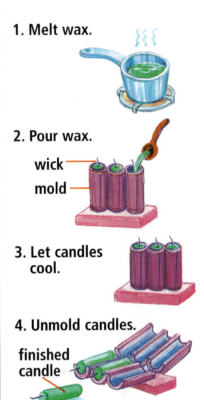

1. Melt wax.

2. Pour wax.
   wick
   mold

3. Let candles cool.

4. Unmold candles.
   finished candle

*These pictures show the **process** of making a candle.*

---

professional

(pru-**fesh**-u-nul) *adjective*

A **professional** worker is someone who gets paid to do a job.

*This **professional** golfer gets paid when he wins golf games.*

protection
(pru-**tek**-shun) *noun*

Protection keeps a thing safe from harm or danger.

*These sharp quills are **protection** for the porcupine.*

proud
(prowd) *adjective*

You are **proud** when you feel happy about something you did.

*These girls are **proud** because they won the game.*

public
(**pub**-lik) *adjective*

Something is **public** when it is for all the people.

*Everyone in the city can go to this **public** park.*

R

reach
(rēch) *verb*

When you **reach** a place, you get there.

*The hikers **reach** the top of the mountain.*

refuse
(ri-**fūz**) *verb*

When you **refuse** to do something, you will not do it.

*This donkey **refuses** to get up!*

remember
(ri-**mem**-bur) *verb*

You **remember** to do something when you are careful not to forget.

*Jess always **remembers** to feed her cat.*

---

reptile
(**rep**-tīl) *noun*

A **reptile** is an animal with dry, scaly skin. Reptiles lay eggs.

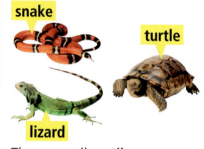

snake
turtle
lizard

*These are all **reptiles**.*

respectful
(ri-**spekt**-ful) *adjective*

When you are **respectful**, you have a high opinion of someone or something.

*These boys are **respectful** of the American flag.*

rocky
(**rok**-ē) *adjective*

A **rocky** place has many rocks and stones.

*It is hard to walk on a **rocky** trail.*

root

(rūt) *noun*

A **root** is the part of a plant that grows into the ground.

← roots

*The **roots** carry food and water from the soil to the rest of the plant.*

sandy

(**san**-dē) *adjective*

Something is **sandy** when it has a lot of sand, or tiny grains of crushed rock.

*Clean your **sandy** feet before you come in the house!*

search

(surch) *verb*

When you **search**, you look carefully to find something.

*They **search** through the basket for their socks.*

seed

(sēd) *noun*

A **seed** is the part of a plant that can grow to become a new plant.

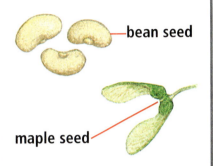

bean seed

maple seed

seedling

(**sēd**-ling) *noun*

A **seedling** is a young plant that grows from a seed.

seedling   **adult plant**

*This **seedling** will grow into an adult pea plant.*

soil

(soil) *noun*

Soil is the dirt plants need in order to grow.

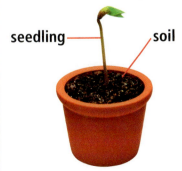

seedling   soil

*Plants need to grow in **soil** that is not too hard or dry.*

spacecraft

(**spās**-kraft) *noun*

People fly in a **spacecraft** to travel in space.

spacecraft

*This **spacecraft** flies above Earth.*

special

(**spesh**-ul) *adjective*

Something **special** is nicer or more important than other things.

*Mom uses the **special** dishes when my grandparents visit.*

start over

(start **ō**-vur) *verb*

When you **start over**, you begin to do something again.

*Carlos had to **start over** when his answer was not correct.*

Statue of Liberty

(**stach**-yū uv **lib**-ur-tē)

proper noun

The **Statue of Liberty** is a statue of a woman holding a torch. It represents the freedom that people have in the United States.

*The **Statue of Liberty** is in New York Harbor.*

stem

(stem) *noun*

The leaves and flowers of a plant grow from the **stem**.

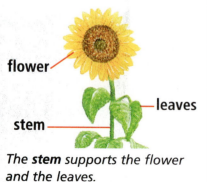

*The **stem** supports the flower and the leaves.*

store

(stor) *verb*

When you **store** something, you keep it until you need it.

*This squirrel **stores** nuts in the tree to eat later, in the winter.*

story

(stor-ē) *noun*

A **story** is a tale about something that happened. It can be real or make-believe.

*It's fun to listen to a **story**!*

strange

(strānj) *adjective*

If something is **strange**, it is different or unusual.

*One zebra has **strange** markings.*

stranger

(strān-jur) *noun*

A **stranger** is someone you do not know.

*The man and woman do not know the **stranger**.*

stretch

(strech) *verb*

When you **stretch**, you make your body longer.

*He stood on tiptoe and **stretched**.*

suffer

(**suf**-ur) *verb*

When you **suffer**, you are uncomfortable or in pain.

*Why does this man **suffer**?*

sunlight
(**sun**-līt) *noun*

Sunlight is the light that comes from the sun.

day   night

Sunlight helps us see things during the day.

supply
(su-**plī**) *verb*

When you **supply** something, you give it what it needs or wants.

You should eat healthy foods to supply your body with nutrients.

surface
(**sur**-fis) *noun*

The **surface** is the outside part of something.

the surface of the Moon

The surface of the Moon is very dry.

symbol
(**sim**-bul) *noun*

A **symbol** is a sign or image that represents an idea or a thing.

The Liberty Bell is a symbol of freedom.

T

together
(tu-**geth**-ur) *adverb*

People are **together** when they are with one another.

together   alone

Lori and Lee read together, but Sonia reads alone.

tracks
(traks) *noun*

Tracks are the marks a person or an animal makes in the ground when it walks.

The tracks of the bear lead to its cave.

U

ugly
(**ug**-lē) *adjective*

If something is **ugly**, it does not look pretty or nice.

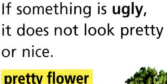
pretty flower

ugly vegetable

What an ugly shape this vegetable has!

understand
(**un**-dur-**stand**) *verb*

When you **understand** something, you know what it means.

Mrs. Garcia helps Huy understand the lesson.

urban
(**ur**-bun) *adjective*

Something that is **urban** has to do with a city.

The city of New York is a large urban area.

valley

(**val**-ē) *noun*

A **valley** is the low place between hills or mountains.

*The mountains rise above this **valley**.*

vegetable

(**vej**-tu-**bul**) *noun*

A **vegetable** is a plant whose roots, stems, or leaves can be used for food.

*Eat **vegetables** everyday to stay healthy.*

visitor

(**viz**-i-tur) *noun*

A **visitor** is someone who goes to see a place or a person for a short period of time.

*The **visitor** is going to stay at the hotel for a week.*

volunteer

(**vol**-un-**tēr**) *noun*

A **volunteer** is someone who does not get paid to do a job.

*This **volunteer** helps at the animal shelter because she loves animals.*

weather

(**weth**-ur) *noun*

When you talk about the **weather,** you talk about what it is like outside.

sunny weather

snowy weather

*Do you like cold or hot **weather**?*

wish for

(wish for) *verb*

You **wish for** something that you want to do or have.

*What do you **wish for**?*

Acknowledgments, continued

Children's Book Press: "My Grandmother's Stories" by Jorge Argueta. Poem copyright © 2002 by Jorge Argueta. Artwork copyright © 2001 by Elizabeth Gomez. Reprinted with the permission of the publisher, Children's Book Press, San Francisco, CA.

Clarion Books/Houghton Mifflin Company: "A Day's Work" cover from *A Day's Work* by Eve Bunting and illustrated by Ronald Hilmer. Reprinted by permission of Clarion Books/Houghton Mifflin Company. All rights reserved.

Crabtree Publishing Company: "How a Plant Grows" by Bobbie Kalman. Reproduced with permission of Crabtree Publishing Company.

Dial Books for Young Readers, a Member of Penguin Putnam Inc.: "Gluskabe and Old Man Winter" from *Pushing Up the Sky* written by Joseph Bruchac and illustrated by Teresa Flavin. Text copyright © Joseph Bruchac, 2000. Illustrations copyright renewed © Teresa Flavin, 2000. Used by arrangement with Dial Books for Young Readers, a member of Penguin Putnam Inc.

Emmett Tenorio Melendez: "My name came from my great-great-great-grandfather" text by Emmett Tenorio Melendez. Use by permission of the author.

Harcourt, Inc.: "Faraway Home" by Jan Kurtz and illustrated by E. B. Lewis. Text copyright © 2000 by Jane Kurtz. Illustrations copyright © 2000 by E. B. Lewis. "A Picnic in October" by Eve Bunting and illustrations by Nancy Carpenter. Text copyright © 1998 by Eve Bunting. Illustrations copyright © 1998 by Nancy Carpenter. Reprinted with permission of Harcourt, Inc.

HarperCollins Publishers: "Central Park Serenade" by Laura Godwin. "December's Song" by Joyce Carol Thomas. Text copyright © 1995 by Joyce Carol Thomas. Illustrations copyright © 1995 by Floyd Cooper. "Good Enough To Eat" by Lizzy Rockwell. Copyright © by Lizzy Rockwell. "Going Home" cover by David Diaz. Jacket art copyright.© 1996 by David Diaz. "I Have An Olive Tree" cover. "In Our One Family" by Arnold Adoff. Text copyright © 1982 by Arnold Adoff. "Love" art by Simon Silva. Illustrations copyright © 1997 by Simon Silva. "Market Day." "Quiet Night" and "Moon" from *Maples in the Mist*. Text copyright © 1996 by Minfong Ho. Illustrations copyright © 1996 by Jean and Mou-Sien Tseng. "Sky Tree" by Thomas Locker. Copyright © 1995 by Thomas Locker. "Strong" art only by Ashley Bryan. Illustration copyright © 2000 by Ashley Bryan. All used by permission of HarperCollins Publishers.

Holiday House, Inc.: "Deserts" from *Deserts* by Gail Gibbons. Copyright © 1996 by Gail Gibbons. All rights reserved. Used by permission of Holiday House, Inc.

Houghton Mifflin Education Place: Quote from Author Biography from Houghton Mifflin Education Place ® Houghton Mifflin Reading, Meet the Illustrator at http://www.eduplace.com/kids/hmr/mtai/carpenter.html © 2001.

Scholastic Inc.: "Lost" adapted from *Lost* by Paul Brett Johnson and Celeste Lewis. Copyright © 1996 by Paul Brett Johnson and Celeste Lewis. Used by permission by Orchard Books, an imprint of Scholastic Inc. "Mice and Beans" from *Mice and Beans* by Pam Muñoz Ryan and illustrated by Joe Cepeda. Copyright © 2001 by Pam Muñoz Ryan and Joe Cepeda. Quote from Pam Munoz Ryan interview from Scholastic Authors Online Library. Copyright © 2001. Quote from book jacket by Joe Cepeda. Reprinted by permission of Scholastic Inc.

Talking Stone Press: "Family Gifts" by Victor Cockburn and Judith Steinbergh from *Where I Come From? Songs and Poems from Many Cultures.* Copyright © 1991. Talking Stone Press, Boston 1991.

Troll Communications L.L.C.: "Dreaming of America" cover from *Dreaming of America: an Ellis Island Story* by Eve Bunting and illustrated by Ben F. Stahl. Illustrations copyright © 2000 by Ben F. Shahl. Published by and reprinted with permission of Troll Communications L.L.C.

Virginia Driving Hawk Sneve: "Another Kid" by Virginia Driving Hawk Sneve.

Photographs:

Altitude: p4 and p12 (Torrance Elementary School, Yann Arthus).

Artville: p485 (apple), p485 (pancakes), p493 (nutrient), p497 (vegetable).

Doug Bekke: p491 (life cycle)

Eve Bunting: p8 and p340 (Eve and father), p341 - p353 (Eve) p360, p363 (Eve).

Cartesia: p485 (map).

Christie's Images: p234 (painting: Charles De Wolf Brownell (1822 - 1909) Oil on Canvas, 1866.

Cidado, Antonio: p124 and 126 (moon phases).

Coleman, Bruce: p488 (fall, Barbara P. Williams), p493 (prey, Warren Photography).

Corbis: p8 and 256 (vulture, George D. Lepp), p14 (rural, James L. Amos), p14 (suburbs, Joseph Sohm/Visions of America), p14 (city, Richard Berebholtz), p15 (Boston City Hall, Todd Gipstein), p67 (water, Bryan Mullennix), p163 (lava flow), p182 (snowy day, James Leynse/SABA), p236 (tree, Randy Wells), p332 (sugar skulls, Charles & Josette Lenars), p333 (Model T, Bettmann), p366 (boy hits pinata, Dianna Sarto), p367 (mother and daughter, Ronnie Kaufman/corbisstockmarket.com), p367 (family party, Rob Lewine/The Stock Market), p408 (father measuring, Bob Jacobson), p416 (water pouring into glass, Michael Neveux), p428 (Ramadan, Annie Griffiths), p428 (Chinese New Year, Phil Schermeister), p460 (family) p466 (family) p480 (Miao girl, Keren Su). Corel p8 (woodpecker, desert, flowering cactus), p44 (grass), p46 (flowers), p50 (leavs), p56-58 (grass), p58 (ruler), p65 (plant life), p92 (vegetable garden), p220 (snapping turtle), p106 (moss), p109 (evergreen tree), p110 (dirt), p113 (helicopter), p114 (grapes), p115 (pine tree), p117 (trees), p118 (all photos), p120 (hollyhocks), p122 (dirt), p229 (nesting birds), p236 (clouds), p240 (flowering cactus), p240 (desert background), p242 (flowering cactus, scorpion, desert eco system, mountain lion), p249 (sandy and rocky desert), p253 (desert wildflowers), p255 (all photos), p256 (woodpecker), p258 (jackrabbit and coyotes), p259 (all photos), p294 (desert), p405 (apples), p406 (orange), p457 (flamingo) p490 (immigrant), p490 (journey, Bettmann), p489 (gully, David Muench), p493 (professional, Duomo), p490 (island, M. Dillon) p489 (garden, Michael Boys), p491 (mayor, Roger Ressmeyer), p494 (respectful, William Gottlieb).

Corel: p46 (flower background, Corel), p118 (trees background), p242 (flowering Sonoran cactus), p242 (Scorpion), p242 (desert Eco System).

Cravath, Lynne: p491 (leave).

Dan Suzio: p102 (Seedlings).

Dwight Kuhn: p5 and p104 (bean sprout), p102 (sprouts below ground), p104 (sunflower), p112 (duckling).

Dan Suzio: p102 (sprouts of sunflowers above ground, Dan Suzio).

Digital Stock: p485 (flowers), p496 (Statue of Liberty)

John Paul Endress Photography: p4 (iceskaters), p40 (sailing and buggy ride), p43 (bridge in Cental Park), p44 (reading), p45 (runners), p46 (dog walker), p47 (Alice in Wonderland), p48 (buggy ride), p49 and p62 (erhu player), p50 (ice skaters), p51 (grounds keeping), p53 (lady in wheelchair).

Getty Images: p1 (sandstone arch), p5 (sunflower), p5 and p64 (ladybug, Christoph Burki), p8 and p296 (ireland, Aldo Torelli), p10 and p410 (spaghetti dinner), p40 (daffodils), p42 (Manhattan skyline, Jake Rajs), p48 (cobblestone), p52 (bricks), p64 (sunflower), p67 (sun, Steve Krongard), p67 (air), p67 (Soil), p94 (background), p106 (sprout in soil, Skip Nall), p106 (White Sands, AZ, Yva Momatiuk), p106 (redwood sorrel, Laurance B. Aiuppy), p109 (prickly pear cactus and carrots), p110 (clouds), p113 (dandelion seed and parachute), p113 (maple seeds, John Warden), p113 (sprouting coconut, Darryl Torckler), p114 (apple sauce, Martin Jacobs), p114 (banana tree, StockTrek), p114 (banana, peanuts, wheat field, apple tree and pine forest), p115 (chair, picnic table, red t-shirt, cotton plant and jeans), p157 (astronaut on the Earth's Moon), p167 (Dave Scott on the Moon), p182 (school supplies), p182 and p366 (note book, Carl Glover), p183 (icy sidewalk), p184 (oak tree, Walter Schmid), p185 (forest in winter), p224 (squirrels, Chris Johns), p246 (Monument Valley, and all cactus), p248 (Monument Valley), p250 (sand dune with grass, Charles C. Place/Image Bank), p250 (Death Valley), p251 (desert), p252 (cactus), p262 (Monument Valley), p264 (desert), p298 (all photos), p299 (U.S. Flag, Statue of Liberty and eagle), p299 (Liberty Bell, Reza Estakhrian), p340 (photo corners and deckled edge), p358 (American flag, clouds and bald eagle), p364 (food pyramid, John Kelly), p404 (doctor, Chabruken), p404 (vegetables), p406 (ice cream, cake, peas, meat, broccoli, and beans), p408 (apple), p409 (children running, Laurence Monneret), p410 (glass of water and salad), p411 (cheese), p412 (oatmeal, Steve Cohen), p413 (girl, Amos Morgan), p414, p415, p423 and p424 (all photos), p428 (parent with daughter), p428 (Thanksgiving dinner, Ryan McVay), p428 (Polynesian dancers, James P. Blair), p428 (campers), p429 (lighting Hanukkah candles, Bushnell/Soifer), p429 (Day of the Dead, Lawrence Migdale), p429 (mother and son, Ross Anania), p480 (Russian kids, James Balog) p487 (desert, Nobert Rosing/National Geographic), p494 (reach, Alexander Stewart/The Image Bank), p498 (vegetable, Anthony Johnson/The Image Bank), p498 (valley, Gary Yeowell/ Stone), p487 (dune, Joe Cornish/Stone), p486 (canyon, Ken Samuelson/PhotoDisc), p486 (community, Patrick Molnar/Taxi), p494 (public, Patti McConville/The Image Bank), p492 (mountain, Russell Illig/PhotoDisc).

Ray Godfrey: p492 (menu.)

Grosshauser, Peter: p485 (branch), p486 (spring), p486 (fall), p486 (summer), p486 (winter).

Hulton Archive: p300 (Statue of Liberty;B&W, Lawrence Thornton), p338 (Statue of Liberty, Lawrence Thorton).

499

Hutchings Photography: p362 (kid in fruit, Richard and Amy Hutchings).

Index Stock: p494 (rocky, Charlie Borland).

Index Stock Imagery: p429 (weaving, Branson Reynolds/Index Stock Imagery).

Ken Karp Photography: p102 (seeds in a jar), p209 (hand with pot lid), p241 (pouring water), p337 (interview), p426 (locket).

Dwight R. Kuhn: p104 (bean sprout), p112 (duckling), p102 (sprouts below ground).

Library of Congress: p426 (female in locket, Library of Congress), p426 (male in locket, Library of Congress).

Map Resource: p59 (Miami map).

Masterfile: p38 (Central Park, Greg Stott), p182 (winter background, ©Roland Weber/Masterfile).

Merlin-net.com p15 (City Council meeting, The Boston Globe).

Metaphotos: p494 (snake), p494 (reptile).

Paul Mirocha: p486 (cloud), p489 (hill).

Peter Mirtschin: p255 (snake).

Francisco X. Mora: p487 (dream).

NASA/Johnson Space Center: p6 (astronaut in suit), p127 (first rocket, astronauts, space station), p129 (spacecraft), p160 (Moon), p160 (Moon Valley), p161 (mountain), p162 (crater), p165 (astronaut in suit), p166 (footprint), p176 (Moon).

Nativestock: p468 and 477 (moccasins, Maralyn "Angel" Wynn/nativestock).

New Century: p485 (sponge), p485 (sponge), p485 (peanuts).

Anthony Nex: p296, p336 and p339 (Eve Bunting, Anthony Nex).

Object Gear: p497 (symbol).

PhotoDisc: p485 (astronaut), p485 (breeze), p488 (experience), p488 (flower), p491 (melt), p492 (nature), p493 (possible), p494 (reptile), p494 (reptile), p495 (soil), p495 (spacecraft), p497 (surface).

PhotoEdit: p486 (city council, Gary Spencer), p488 (ferry, Deborah Davis), p494 (remember, Amy Etra), p489 (helpful, Cindy Charles), p490 (important), p496 (story, David Young-Wolff), p489 (government), p497 (urban, Jeff Greenberg).

Photo Researchers, Inc.: p8 and p256 (elf owl in nest Organ Pipe National Monument, Peter B. Kaplan/Photo Researchers, Inc.), p254 (Western Diamond Back Rattlesnake, Stephen Dalton/Photo Researchers, Inc.), p487 (dangerous, Rafael Macia).

PictureQuest: p429 (Kawanzaa celebration, Joe Atlas/ Brand X), p480 (girl, Ann Cecil/ Photo 20-20), p480 (boy, Tony Freeman/PhotoEdit), p453 (grandmother and grandchild, Digital Vision), p429 (baseball practice, Keith Brofsky/ Brand X), p489 (frost, Peter Lilja/Pictor International, Ltd.).

Richard L. Roe: p19 (Davie, Florida aerial, Courtesy Richard L. Roe).

Schwartz, Carol: p495 (root)

Science Photo Library: p486 (crater, NASA).

Shepherd, Roni: p486 (convince), p487 (disappear), p488 (energy), p488 (faraway), p488 (forget), p489 (found), p490 (idea), p490 (imagine), p490 (impossible), p491 (lost), p492 (mineral), p492 (neighborhood), p493 (process), p494 (protection), p494 (refuse), p495 (sandy), p495 (search), p495 (seed), p495 (seedling), p495 (special), p495 (start over), p496 (stem), p496 (store), p496 (strange), p496 (stranger), p496 (suffer), p497 (tracks), p498 (visitor), p498 (weather), p498 (wish).

Stockbyte: p497 (pretty flower).

SuperStock, Inc.: p26 and p300 (Statue of Liberty, Steve Vidler/Super Stock).

The Boston Globe / Merlin-net.com: p15 (city council meeting, the Boston Globe).

Viesti Associates Inc: p488 (family, Martha Cooper).

Liz Garza Williams: p485 (adapt), p485 (came from), p486 (connect), p487 (decision), p487 (diet), p488 (envelope), p489 (healthy), p490 (homesick), p490 (astronaut), p491 (meal), p492 (memory), p492 (memory), p494 (proud), p496 (stretch), p497 (sunlight), p497 (night), p497 (supply), p497 (together), p497 (together), p497 (understand), 498 (volunteer).

Author and Illustrator Photos:

p31 (Courtesy of Raúl Colón), p52 (John Paul Endress), p55 (Dion Ogust), p95 (Grace Lin, Courtesy of Grace Lin), p149 (Francisco X. Mora), p205 (Courtesy of Michael Greenlar), p231 (Courtesy of Neefus Photographers), p261 (Courtesy of Gail Gibbons), p287 (Courtesy of Diane Lawless), p329 (Courtesy of Nancy Carpenter), p397 (Courtesy of Pam Muñoz Ryan), p452 (Courtesy of E. B. Lewis). p465 (Theresa Kennett), p467 (Carl Wolinsky), p469 (Courtesy V.D.H. Sneve), p471 (Barbara Goldberg), p475 (Steve Anderson).

Illustrations:

JoLynn Alcorn: p413 (digestive system); **Amy Bates:** pp430-431; **Annie Bissett:** maps pp19, 271, 303, 433; **Raúl Colón:** p4 (center), pp18-31, p33; **Lisa Chapman:** p66; **Floyd Cooper:** pp472-475; **Simon Galkin:** pp470-471; **Morissa Geller:** p103; **Patrick Gnan:** pp107-108 (parts of a plant); p246 (cross-section of cactus), p252 (cross-section of cactus), p257; **Diane Greenseid:** pp336-337; **Eileen Hine:** p422; **Daryl Ligasan:** pp268-269; **Maurie Manning:** pp70-95, pp96-97, pp98-99 (border), p99 (top); **Geoffrey McCormack:** p15; **Patrick Merrell:** pp42-43, p58 (bottom map); **Sherry Nedigh:** p292; **Karen Patcau:** pp16-17; **Sebastian Quigley:** p158 (craters on Earth), p162 (craters on Earth), p260; **Lizzy Rockwell:** p60; **Robert Roper:** pp212-213; **Stacey Schuett:** 68-69; **Pablo Torrecilla:** p07 (center), pp184-205, pp206-207, pp208-209 (border);

The Avenues Development Team

Hampton-Brown extends special thanks to those who contributed so much to the creation of the Grade 3, 4, and 5 Pupil Editions.

Editorial: Janine Boylan, Julie Cason, Lisa Cittadino, Shirleyann Costigan, Phyllis Edwards, Roseann Erwin, Nadine Guarrera, Margot Hanis, Fredrick Ignacio, Cynthia Keith, Phillip Kennedy, Tiina Kurvi, Sheron Long, S. Michele McFadden, Amy Ostenso, Heather Peacock, Sharon Ursino, and Cullen Wojcik.

Design and Production: Renae Arcinas, Katherine A. Butler, Christy Caldwell, Jen Coppens, Sherry Corley, Jeri Gibson, Terry Harmon, Rick Holcomb, Connie McPhedran, Michael Moore, Russ Nemec, Marian O'Neal, Anthony Paular, Cathy Revers, Augustine Rivera, Debbie Saxton, DJ Simison, Curtis Spitler, Jonni Stains, Debbie Swisher, Vicki Vandeventer, Elvin (JR) Walker, and Bill Smith Studios.

Permissions: Barbara Mathewson